COMPUTER LITERACY

D1456483

COMPUTER LITERACY

The Basic Concepts and Language

JOHN V. LOMBARDI

INDIANA UNIVERSITY PRESS
Bloomington

Manufactured in the United States of America

Library of Congress Cataloging in Publication Data

Lombardi, John V.
   Computer literacy.

   Includes index.
   1. Computer literacy. I. Title.
QA76.9.C64L65 1983   001.64   83-48122
ISBN 0-253-31401-1
ISBN 0-253-21075-5 (pbk.)
1 2 3 4 5 87 86 85 84 83

For David W. Davies

Contents

Preface

This book is the result of the efforts of many people, primarily at Indiana University and in the Bloomington community, who have given their time and expertise to my quest for the perfect computer. Some have been patient and tolerant, explaining the obvious with grace and charm. Others, irritated by the brash neophyte in their midst, dismissed my poorly put queries with ill-disguised contempt. Fortunately, the charmers have much outnumbered the others, and I, too, acquired some computer literacy.

The ranks of the neophytes have been greatly expanded by the appearance of the affordable, powerful microcomputer, and this book is directed to them. Their questions echo mine, and the starting points provided here are those that helped me most when I began. With the language and basic concepts of computer literacy mastered, anyone can ask the right questions and get useful answers.

A special debt of gratitude goes to Indiana University's Bloomington Academic Computing Services, a dedicated group of professionals whose staff, whether at the Marshal H. Wrubel Computing Center or elsewhere on campus, has tolerated my questions and corrected my errors for over a decade. Those who have helped are too many to list here, but I wouldn't have known where to start without them. In the Bloomington community, I have relied often on

Ray Borrill during his long tenure as founder and manager of The Data Domain, and on John Prather of RCA and president of our local Apple user's group.

A number of colleagues have read this book and found most of the errors or contributed in other ways. My thanks to Bobbie Adams, George Alter, John Buck, Paul Dawson, Dan DeHayes, Jerry McIntosh, Jerry Olsen, Ed Robertson, and John Smith. In addition, the editorial staff of the IU Press gave me even more than their normal high-quality care and advice.

This book is dedicated to David W. Davies, who patiently explained why a humanist should pay attention to computers, and this in 1967 when we all thought Apples grew on trees. As librarian, historian, and friend, David W. Davies has always been an inspiration.

As always, my family supported this effort. The children let me use the computers once in a while, and my wife, Cathryn Lee Lombardi, endured my infatuation with the machine and even contributed the diagrams in this book.

To all of them, my thanks.

COMPUTER LITERACY

I Computer Literacy for Adults

Two buzz words of our time: Computer Literacy. They appear in popular magazines, on the agendas of Parent Teacher Organizations, in the catalogs of our colleges, and in the learned columns of professional journals. In the manner of all such quick substitutes for thought, the notion of computer literacy can mean anything.

Elementary school parents and teachers think it means familiarity with microcomputers and the ability to turn one on and off without damaging the machine. University computer science faculty think it means the ability to program in at least three computer languages, comprehend the elements of computer architecture, and understand the fundamentals of Boolean logic. Computer literacy is all of these things and everything in between.

Before allowing anyone to talk about computer literacy, then, ask two questions: Computer literacy for what purpose? Computer literacy for whom?

This book is for adults who have graduated from high school and probably college, who have an interest in computers, and who are willing to spend some time finding out about them.

This book provides enough information about microcomputers for adults to understand general articles about the machines and their impact, to feel confident enough to turn one of them on and off, to begin learning how to do word processing tasks, to understand how to prepare a financial or mathematical table, and to have a general understanding of what computer programming is and how it is accomplished.

This book starts from the premise that computer literacy means the ability to recognize problems for which the computer may be a useful part of the solution. Computer literate adults will be able to identify appropriate computer resources for a wide range of tasks and they will know how to ask the experts for assistance in finding solutions using computers.

Those who are not interested in microcomputers should stop reading here and find another book. But if you are not interested, you should be.

Microcomputers are ubiquitous. They turn up everywhere. But it is not the little computer in your microwave oven, your TV, or your car that commands your attention and recommends computer literacy to you. Instead, it is the word processor in your office, the microcomputer used by your accountant or publisher, and the game machines coveted by your children that will force you to do one of two things.

Either you will become literate enough to know what these machines can do and when they should be avoided, or you will have to continue to pretend that it doesn't matter. However, it does matter, and if you don't understand, someone else will make many decisions for you in the name of computers.

Computers, marvelously complex and mysterious machines, are no more difficult to understand than your dishwasher or your car.

2

You don't need to know much about mechanical engineering to understand what dishwashers do, how to make them do it, and what tasks they help perform. You don't have to comprehend the intricacies of a gasoline engine to know that the automobile has changed our lives, rearranged our landscape, and captured significant parts of our income. You can understand cars and dishwashers well enough to have an opinion about what to do with them. Computer literacy equips you to approach the computer in the same way.

Your children will not need this book, but unless you are ready to quit, you do.

Why Begin with Microcomputers?

Why not talk about big computers? They are powerful, they control our bank accounts, our military establishment, our economy, and the IRS. They are the machines that manage our credit card accounts, print our payroll checks, and calculate the trajectory of space ships. Are they not more important?

Not for me, and probably not for you. You don't have a chance to do much with such machines. You don't have the opportunity to manage them, control them, or put them to work for you. They exist, cared for by the acolytes of computerese who often appear reluctant to make it easy for you to understand or control the big computers.

Microcomputers, however, are cheap and small. They exist as individual units that can be turned on and off by you. They are in your office or school, they are sold in retail stores like television sets or expensive stereos. You can buy one, take it home, plug it in, and make it type your correspondence, prepare your taxes, or plan your budget. You can have it in the office to calculate budget reports, organize mailing lists, prepare progress reports, type books or newsletters, and do a host of other useful and interesting things.

These microcomputers have amazing power equivalent to what used to take a house with superior air conditioning to enclose. You can buy one in a small box with a small tv screen for less than half the price of a new car. That is why you need to know about microcomputers.

Also, although the acolytes of the big computers don't want you to think so, most of what you will learn to do with microcomputers is practically the same as what they do, only they do it bigger, if not always better. So for you and me, it is the micro-computer that is important.

How to Become Computer Literate

It doesn't much matter how you become computer literate. You can go out and buy a microcomputer, take it home, plug it in, read the manual, and become computer literate. Many of us did it that way. It is reasonably inefficient, and for adults, often very frustrating.

Your children probably have an entirely different approach to computer literacy. I've often tried to explain, in a logical orderly fashion, all about microcomputers to my own children ages 11 and 14. They listen politely for a short while and then proceed to jump completely ahead of my explanation, turn the thing on, and make it do what they wanted it to do.

They may, sometime in the future, have a clear academic knowledge of computers, but right now, they just make the computer do what they want. When it doesn't behave as expected, they ask me what to do,

I tell them, and they continue. The goal of this book is to get you where you can at least converse with an average 14 year old.

Adults generally like the world structured and organized in some logical way. It helps us learn and understand. So in the book, we will approach the microcomputer in a series of logical steps.

First, there is the machine itself. The market is full of microcomputers. Each manufacturer offers special and complex features, tells us that each machine is wonderfully unique and unlike any other machine since the beginning of time (about 1973).

That is bunk. Most microcomputers are something on the order of 90% the same. Moreover, most of the differences are so technical and frequently trivial that only computer gurus care.

As a result, the first thing to do in a book on computer literacy is to build a prototypical micro-computer. This makes it relatively easy to discuss the major parts of these machines and explain what they do and why you need to know about them. It provides the occasion for an explanation of opera-ting systems. And it will introduce you to the wonderful jargon of computerese. One of the deli-cious benefits of computer literacy is the mastery of a new idiom, a set of words and phrases that imply consummate technical sophistication but refer to quite ordinary and mundane things.

Of course, once the microcomputer is built, we need to do something useful with it; after all, that is the point of the exercise. So the next logical topic of this book on computer literacy is word pro-cessing.

Word processing is nothing more complicated than

typing words on electronic paper, rearranging them to look pretty, checking the spelling, and having them typed onto real paper. But if we said all that, no one would be impressed, so we call it word processing.

Word processing is a practically universal use of microcomputers. In the beginning, not to frighten people, the makers of these microcomputers called their machines Word Processors so that no one would catch on that they were really computers moving words around. Now that everyone wants a computer, all the word processing companies advertise their machines as microcomputers or, if they are especially clever, work processors. In any case, one of the most useful things a computer can do for you is manage words.

After words, the next most popular thing to do with computers is manage numbers. Computers do numbers very well indeed, and for a while, some people thought that was all the computer could do.

Computers have many complicated and confusing ways to manage numbers, but the microcomputer has been made a major consumer appliance by the invention of what is called a spreadsheet calculator. This is an electronic page divided into rows and columns. The page is very large. You can put numbers in rows or columns or both. You can add, subtract, multiply, or divide these numbers in any way you want. You can combine two rows and put them in a third, you can move, modify, and otherwise change these numbers in rows and columns in any way that makes you happy.

Most of us spend a lot of time moving numbers around this way. Our budgets and tax records, our accounts and planning exercises, all use arrangements of numbers in rows and columns. So the electronic spreadsheet has become one of the most popular tools that requires a microcomputer to work, and spreadsheets have sold more microcomputers than even Space Invaders. Spreadsheets are the next subject of computer literacy.

While the individualistic nature of the micro-computer--the personal computer of advertising lore--is one of its most attractive features, most people will sooner or later want to connect their machine to something bigger or at least to another microcomputer. When you connect two microcomputers you have a network, and when you have a network you are engaged in computer communications. So another major topic of computer literacy is communications. Computer communications turn out to be almost as difficult as human communications with misunder-standing and confusion rampant. However, the major characteristics of the process and the simple solu-tions are quite accessible.

Finally, everyone needs to know something about programming. This is not to say that everyone must be a programmer, or even that every computer liter-ate person needs to be able to write any program. Not at all. But because a program is what makes the computer worth the trouble, it helps to understand the process.

The program is the set of instructions that make the computer help you rearrange your words or num-bers the way you want them. If the program is good, the computer will make it easy and fast to do the rearranging. If it is bad, you will want to go back to a pencil.

For some reason, the technical ingenuity required to invent computing machinery is more prolific and rapid than the creativity required for programming. This genetic phenomenon results in better, faster, more powerful machines long before there are any instructions to make them do anything useful. Computer literacy requires some knowledge of what programming is, how it is done, and why it is harder than it looks.

This, then, completes the outline of what I think it takes to be computer literate. Everyone has a different definition, but if you stay with this book, you'll learn enough to demonstrate that I am wrong.

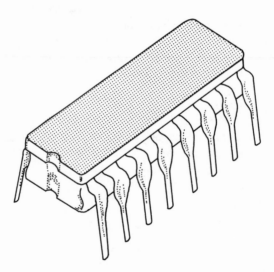

Computer Chip

II Microcomputer: The Machine

This part of the book indulges in a reasonably large amount of jargon. While good style might eliminate such words and phrases, computer literacy would not be served.

If you want to converse with computers or computer people, you must understand their technical language. It turns out to be easier to learn their jargon than to try to communicate with them normally. A glossary is included at the end of the book, but when you discover how simple the definitions of these words actually are, you probably won't need it.

Every microcomputer is made up of the same parts that do essentially the same things. Companies package these parts differently, sometimes for good effect and sometimes to make you think that the old stuff is really new. If you know all the parts, it is relatively easy to know when a sales representative is trying to impress you with ordinary things.

The heart of every microcomputer is an electronic device known as a microprocessor. This chip of plastic, loaded with circuits, looks like a rectangular bug with two rows of legs. The legs, of course, are wires that connect the microprocessor to the rest of the computer. Everything else in the computer is organized to serve the microprocessor, and the power of the computer is limited by the power of this chip.

These microprocessors go by many names--or numbers. The Apple computer, for example, has a 6502 microprocessor and Radio Shack has a Z80, some have a 68000, and others have an 8088. The gurus of microcomputer can discourse endlessly about the advantages and disadvantages of each of these chips, but for the most part, it doesn't make much difference. The arguments only make sense after you know what you want the computer to do, and then you can find out if the Z80 or the 6502 can do it. Nine times out of ten they both can, and the difference between them is on the order of a fraction of a second.

Every microprocessor has a set of instructions built into its circuits that allow it to add, subtract, or move information. Unfortunately, each microprocessor has a slightly different set of instructions to do the same things so that the programs and machines are not easily interchangeable.

Microprocessors, however, rarely can do anything useful by themselves. They can calculate, but they can't remember very much. They can move information, but they have no place to keep it. And of course, there is no way for you to tell it what to do or for it to tell you the result.

So the first thing our computer needs is memory. Memory gives the microprocessor someplace to store information and instructions. It provides storage for the work waiting to be done, the instructions for doing it, and the results when it is done. Most microcomputers have quite a lot of this memory, usually enough to store about 64,000 numbers or letters. In jargon, this is called 64K of memory.

This memory comes in two varieties. The first variety is permanent memory. That is memory that will keep its information even if the computer is turned off. This kind of memory, because it is permanent, can be read only. The microprocessor can read what is in this memory, but because it is permanent, the microprocessor cannot write anything into this memory, otherwise it would write over what was already there and erase it. The result is that computer people call this Read Only Memory, or ROM for short. Most microcomputers have something on the order of 10,000 to 60,000 characters of ROM. This ROM normally has instructions that tell the microprocessor how to manage the rest of the microcomputer, and because the computer must always know these instructions, we keep them in permanent memory, in ROM.

The rest of the computer's memory is quite volatile. The microprocessor can write information into that memory and then read it back. It can erase it, move it, and in general do anything it has instructions to do with information in that memory. This memory is organized to allow the microprocessor, given a memory location or address, to fetch the information from anywhere in this memory without reading through any other part of memory.

For example, I can tell the microprocessor to get the letter stored at the 34,000th location in memory and move it to the 45,000th place. The microprocessor will go immediately to 34,000, fetch the letter, and copy it into 45,000. This ability to read and write anywhere in the memory in one step is called random access. That means that given any random sequence of memory locations, the microprocessor can go directly to each one whether they are in order or not. Such a memory has the name Random Access Memory, or RAM for short.

The combination of ROM and RAM gives the computer its complement of internal memory. The amount of memory that can be accessed directly by the microprocessor is a function of the microprocessor's design. These devices are classified in part by the amount of data they can move at one time.

Microcomputers such as the Apple II and the Radio Shack TRS-80 IV can move data one character at a time. The microprocessor sees each of these characters as a number made up of 8-bits. The bit is a value that can be either on or off, 1 or 0. The way most of these 8-bit machines are designed, they can directly manage about 64K of memory.

However, newer microprocessors can move more data at a time because they get their information in two-character pieces or 16-bit chunks. Their design permits the direct management of as much as a million bytes of memory.

In theory, a 16-bit microprocessor is better than an 8-bit microprocessor, but in practice the only thing that counts is whether the microcomputer does what you want it to do, not whether it does it 8 or 16-bits at a time.

The combination of 8-bits is called a byte, and a byte is a unit of computer information that is roughly equivalent to one letter or character of the alphabet. Hence, a memory of 64K (bytes) can hold over 64,000 characters or about 13,000 words.

All this memory is wonderful because it gives the microprocessor someplace to get information and someplace to put information. Unfortunately, we still need a way to talk to the microprocessor and to put information into or take it out of memory. These important activities are done through keyboards, display screens, disk drives, and other

12

devices I'll talk about in a minute. But first we have to be able to connect these things to the memory and the microprocessor.

There are any number of ways to attach keyboards, screens, and other equipment to the microprocessor and memory. All of them use some variant of a bus.

Now a computer bus is not a motor vehicle but rather a systematic collection of wires whose purpose is to collect incoming information and route it through the microprocessor to memory and to take the outgoing information and route it through the microprocessor to a screen or other external device.

Microcomputers such as the Apple II and the IBM PC have what are called open buses because they have arranged their equipment in such a way that it is easy to plug devices into the bus. The instructions provided the microcomputer determine to which device on the bus the microprocessor will listen or speak.

The two minimal devices that we will have to connect to the bus so that we can make this microcomputer do something useful are a keyboard and a display screen or monitor. The keyboard is a very straightforward typewriter style item, sometimes with extra keys to make the computer do interesting things. The monitor is a tv screen that displays whatever a program's instructions tell the microprocessor to display, usually the results of some activity or a request for some information.

Now, finally, we have a functioning microcomputer. Just plug it in, and away we go. We'll write in some instructions, do some work, and see the results on the screen. Unfortunately, when we want to quit for the day and turn the thing off, all our instructions and results disappear because the RAM does not keep anything intact when the power is off. So it seems we'll need to do more with this computer before it becomes useful.

The next addition will be a disk drive. This is akin to a record player except that the record it plays is made of a thin, flexible disk of mylar plastic with the kind of magnetic coating found on tape recorder tape. The disk, called a floppy disk in the trade, lives in a square cardboard jacket that protects it from hazards like fingers and dust.

On instruction from the computer, the disk drive can read information from the disk and write information onto the disk. This disk drive functions as a type of external storage, and it can hold lots more information than memory. Most microcomputers have disk drives that use 5-1/4" floppy disks, and each of these disks can hold from 100,000 (100K) to 500K numbers or letters. The information stored in this fashion can be kept safely long after the computer is turned off.

Now, we can do some work with our computer and when we are done we can have the computer tell the disk drive to store the instructions, the information, and the results in safe and permanent storage on the magnetic disk placed in the disk drive. If we use up all the space on one of these disks, we take it out, put in another one, and continue until our work is done. When we no longer need the information saved on a disk, we can erase it and use it again. Very convenient.

Sometimes two disk drives are helpful if we have lots of information on one disk and we want to do something to it and put it on another disk. With two disk drives we can handle both the original disk and the resulting disk conveniently. For this reason, serious microcomputers have two disk drives.

14

This microcomputer is now becoming rather interesting and useful. But when I want to send the results of my work to a friend or discuss it with a colleague, I don't want to carry my computer across town, and they can't tell what is on my disks without a clone of my computer. So it would be very nice to be able to put the results of my work on paper. The device? A printer of course. It, too, can be plugged into the bus and receive information from the computer. However, unlike the disk drives, the printer is strictly an output device; it does not send information to the computer, it only receives information from the computer.

Printers come in a bewildering variety: large, small, fast, slow, fancy, plain, color, black and white, dot matrix, letter-quality. Ah yes, jargon again. What heady stuff!

Dot matrix is a fancy name for printers that make their characters, letters, numbers, or whatever with lots of little dots. If there are enough dots, the letter looks almost solid. The virtue of these printers is that they tend to be inexpensive, are very flexible, offer many different type styles and graphics features, and are quite fast. However, the quality of the letters and numbers they produce is not as good as what you get from a high quality electric typewriter.

So the second category of printer is what is known as a letter quality printer. These use type elements of varying design but produce exactly the same or better quality as any electric typewriter. They tend to be slower, less flexible, and more durable than the dot matrix printers. They also tend to be much more expensive.

15

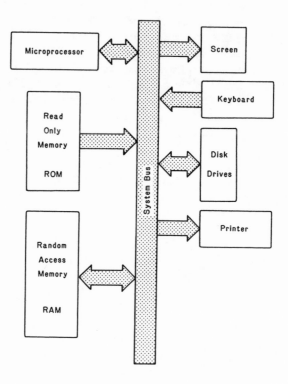

Basic Microcomputer Hardware

In any event, with keyboard, screen, disk drives, and printer attached, we have a complete and functioning microcomputer system. This machine can currently be purchased for about $2,500. It is capable of doing high quality word processing. It can handle very sophisticated numbers, whether for accounting purposes, budgeting, engineering, education, or scientific study. It is, in short, a very powerful tool.

This microcomputer can also be connected to a wide variety of other accessories that make it even more useful for special purposes. Some people need elaborate designs, and this microcomputer can instruct a plotter to draw pictures, maps, diagrams, charts, and the like. It can connect you to big computers or other small computers.

Microcomputers can do many tasks, they can be made to operate a wide range of devices, but to accomplish these things, they need quality instructions. In the end, the computer is no smarter or more able than the instructions provided it.

To understand how the computer gets and uses these instructions to accomplish useful work we must start with a special set of instructions called the operating system that handles all the housekeeping chores involved in managing disk drives, keyboards, screens, printers, and other devices. It is the machine's supervisor, and the functions it performs are essential. Indeed, the operating system is frequently more important than the microprocessor itself in determining how useful and accessible your computer will be.

Operating systems, like everything else in the microcomputer business, come in many varieties. These complex programs have two faces. The first face is the one you see on the screen. It tells you when the computer is ready to work, it asks you for information, it tells you what is on the disks in your drive, and it can provide you with many useful functions to help you manage all that hardware. Some operating systems can show you much the same face, no matter what the microprocessor inside the computer. Indeed, there is some tendency for various operating systems to try to look alike, even if their other faces are very different.

The other face of the operating system you will rarely see. It is designed to speak to the specific hardware installed in your machine or attached to it. As a result, it must be very precise about what your equipment can and cannot do, how it prefers to have it done, and what instructions are required to make it perform. These specifications differ not only between computers with different microprocessors but also between computers with the same microprocessor but with slightly different arrangements of disks, keyboards, or screens.

Fortunately, most applications programs, programs that actually do something for you such as word processing, are designed to use only the face that you see. Thus a word processing program that will run on a specific operating system in one computer will probably run equally well on the same operating system installed in another computer, even if this machine has a much different kind of disk drive. For this reason, when choosing a microcomputer, you need to learn which operating systems will work on that machine and what applications programs will be available to you with the operating system.

Operating systems come in two main varieties: generic and proprietary.

The generic operating system is one designed to work on a number of different manufacturer's computers. Three of these deserve some introduction here.

Control Program/Microcomputers, universally known as CP/M (pronounced C-P-M), probably holds the record as the most generic of all operating systems. Designed to manage the resources of microcomputers based on the Z-80 microprocessor (and other compatible chips), this venerable operating system has the largest base of applications software. That means more programs to do something useful can be run under the control of CP/M than any other generic operating system.

This operating system is best known to users for the cryptic nature of its comments and the obscurity of its commands. Indeed, many enterprising programmers make a living from programs designed to give CP/M a prettier face. However, even though CP/M is somewhat plain in appearance, it is a superb performer. The operating system flexibly manages microcomputer memory, disks, printers, and other resources with considerable ease. Its popularity stems not from the face presented to the user, but the flexibility and capacity it affords programmers. The operating system is venerable, stable, and likely to be around for a long time. Its existence and the huge base of software that uses it will guarantee the life span of Z-80 compatible microprocessors long after they are technologically obsolete.

With the advent of 16-bit microprocessors, new operating systems had to be developed to manage the interconnection of devices, memory, and other gadgets with the new microprocessor. CP/M rose to the challenge with something called, not very imaginatively, CP/M-86. That means Control Program/Microcomputer for the 8086/8088 family of microprocessors. An 8088 is the computer chip that is in the IBM Personal Computer, among others.

CP/M-86 wears the same face toward the user, making the transition from a CP/M machine to a CP/M-86 machine virtually painless. However, as you would expect, the face toward the computer chips is completely changed in order to take advantage of the superior power and flexibility of the new microprocessor.

CP/M-86's most important competitor in the generic operating system category is MS-DOS, otherwise known as MicroSoft Disk Operating System. MS-DOS is also called PC-DOS when used on the IBM Personal Computer, but it is the same thing. MS-DOS has a face toward the user that looks very similar to CP/M-86, but with enough differences to confuse you if you have to use both. Because of the strong support IBM has given MS-DOS, the betting so far is that MS-DOS may be the winner in the competition with CP/M-86, although many programmers have decided to hedge their bets by making their programs run under either one.

The final generic operating system worth noting here is the University of California San Diego P-system, or UCSD P-system. This is an operating system designed primarily for the Pascal programming language, but due to its versatility and transportability to most microcomputer systems, it has evolved into a generic operating system. Nevertheless, because of its Pascal association, UCSD P-system does not have quite as large a software base as the CP/Ms and MS-DOS. However, it does have the advantage that it runs virtually identically on 8-bit and 16-bit machines.

Proprietary operating systems, unlike the generics, will only work on one manufacturer's computer, even if other computers share the same microprocessor. Thus, the VIC-64 and Apple both use a chip called the 6502, but because they use proprie-

that can be managed with CP/M, in this case the popular Z-80. Such solutions, while often very satisfactory, make sense only if you really need the specialized applications available only with the proprietary operating system, otherwise you are better off with one operating system, and a generic one at that.

In addition to managing the physical resources of a microcomputer, the operating system handles the chores of keeping track of the collections of data and instructions we have saved on floppy disks. These are kept in files. Depending on our particular computer and its operating system, the technical details of how these files of information are kept vary, but there are at least two major distinctions that apply to most systems.

Data files are collections of information, generally stored on disk just as they would be displayed on the screen or printed on paper. If the file is a list of names and addresses, that list is a data file, stored on the disk. When we save it on the disk, we give it a name. And when we want to use it again, the operating system allows us to recall it by name. This is possible because every disk has a directory saved on it (also a file) with the names of all the files and an index to the location of that file's information on the disk.

Program files are also collections of information, but they are usually stored in a special format understood by the machine. Many operating systems make a special distinction between program files and data files, although some do not much care. Usually, you do not have to worry about what kind of file is involved, except to follow the rules outlined in the instructions that accompany your operating system. More sophisticated operating systems such as CP/M and MS-DOS have a number of special file types,

tary operating systems, programs that wo
cannot be run directly on the other. Ra
has a proprietary operating system, as do r
manufacturers. But the proprietary system
largest software base is probably Apple
DOS 3.3. That, of course, is Disk Operati
version 3.3. DOS 3.3 is proprietary to A
other manufacturers of Apple look-alike
have made their machines in such a way tl
DOS will run on their machines.

The virtue of the proprietary operating
that it allows the manufacturer to build d
on a single machine, making a change to
chine difficult if it is not compatible
proprietary system; the software for the ol
will not run on the new machine unless the
common operating system. The disadvantag
most proprietary operating systems do no
much software available as generic opera
tems. Apple is something of a special cas
the software base for this proprietary
system is very large indeed, although pro
as large as the CP/M software base.

Although the size of the software base at
any given operating system can be a useful
of its general acceptance and utility, you
little if the program you need runs under s
operating system. If you want games and
purpose software, a proprietary operatii
such as Apple DOS 3.3 may be perfect, bi
need a wide range of business applications,
will find more help with CP/M or MS-DOS.

Recognizing this problem, clever compu
have invented add-in devices that will a
Apple, for example, to run CP/M. These
simply replace your resident microprocesso
case of the Apple the 6502, with a micro

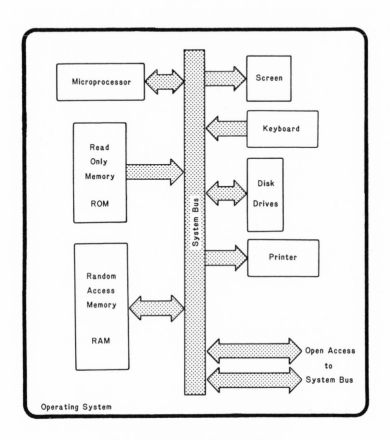

Microcomputer Hardware

with Operating System

each identified by a suffix attached to its name. While the instructions that come with these operating systems tend to make these naming conventions appear very complex, in fact, most activities with the microcomputer do not require a detailed knowledge of all the various file types.

Now that we have hardware, files, and an operating system to manage them, we are ready to get the programs, the quality instructions, that will have the machine doing something useful. This machine, with its operating system, can do an incredible variety of things, given enough quality instructions. Your use of the machine will be limited only by your imagination and the availability of quality instructions.

You will, of course, run out of quality instructions before you run out of imagination, which leads us to the next topic, word processing.

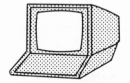

Computer Terminal

III   Word Processing
and Microcomputers

Practically everyone with access to a computer wants it to work like a fancy typewriter, or what is known as a word processor. Our typical microcomputer with its printer, disk drives, keyboard, and other features will, it turns out, make a fine word processing machine. All that is required are the instructions that tell the machine how to behave like an intelligent typewriter. These instructions, naturally, constitute the word processing program.

It is in the nature of the beast that word processing is much more difficult to talk about than it is to demonstrate or do. As a result, when you read about word processing you can get the idea that it is complicated, requires lots of practice, and demands high technical knowledge.

Not so. You need to pay slightly more attention to a word processor than you do to an electric typewriter, but only slightly. The result of this extra attention is a tool that makes the electric typewriter look like hammer, chisel, and stone tablet. Word processing is truly the most generally useful thing that microcomputers can be made to do. More important than numbers, more important than games. Of course, I'm biased, since I mostly work with words.

In any event, you need to know about word processing. So first, let me tell you what I think it is. You will find that academics, computer people, sales representatives, writers, secretaries, publishers, and newspaper editors all have slightly different notions about what word processing is and does. The people who write and sell programs to instruct your microcomputer on how to be a word processor each have their own understanding of what the world's most wonderful word processing program should be able to do.

Given this multiplicity of definitions, the best way to proceed is to invent a typical word processing program for our typical microcomputer. Then, when you see or try a word processor, you will understand the various features and capabilities and how they should work.

There are two major parts to putting words into a computer and getting them back out arranged as you want them. The first is called editing and the second is called formatting.

Editing is the process of typing the words into the computer's memory, correcting the words to be sure they say what you want them to say, rearranging them so they appear in the proper order, and checking them to be sure they are spelled correctly. Editing also includes providing some means for the computer to know how you want the finished letter or article or report to look. Once you have all the words entered into the machine correctly, then you need to get the computer to arrange them pleasingly on the typed page. The arrangement process is called formatting.

Formatting does things like fit the correct number of words on each line, put the right number of lines on each page, start paragraphs where they should be started, place page numbers where you want them, and

26

do the many housekeeping chores required for clean, neat, typed copy.

Good formatting programs do lots of fancy things. They can underline, put text in bold face, change margins mid-page, do hanging indentations, place footnotes at the bottom of the appropriate page, change ribbon color, and in general make your document look just so.

The beauty of the formatting is that the words you type into the machine during the editing phase do not have to be arranged neatly. It is the formatting program that transforms them into clean, neat copy. You can make any number of corrections or add, delete, move and change the text with the editor; the formatter will take this copy and redo its arrangement on the pages effortlessly.

Now, some people like to see just what the page will look like while they enter text, and they want to be able to see how these changes affect the final arrangement of words on the page. They want to have the editing and the formatting take place at the same time. This is called on-screen formatting, or in the more casual parlance of the marketplace "what you see is what you get" word processing. Many of the best word processing programs will accomplish this on-screen formatting while you type the text so that you do not have to imagine what the final page will look like.

Let us then design the typical microcomputer word processing program. First, we'll pick an on-screen formatter with editor, a "what you see is what you get" system, because it is usually easier to use. This program must have several important features.

First, the Help commands. The Help commands will display on the screen information about features and commands of the word processing program so you do not have to refer to a manual in order to know what to do to achieve any special effect or take advantage of the program's capabilities.

Second, we want this word processor to have a full-screen editor. This means that you can jump around anywhere in the text to fix, add, delete, or change anything. You don't have to know what line you are on or what page you are on. You can go anywhere in the text and do what you want. This keeps your screen as much like an electronic piece of paper as possible.

When you work with a pencil, you can scratch out a word, insert a word, cut out paragraphs, move blocks of text around, or otherwise fix the text anywhere, and our word processor should let you do the same. The only difference is that when you fix with the computer you don't have to retype anything that is correct, and the fixes appear as if no change had been made at all.

Third, we want this word processor to be able to handle a lot of text at a time. It will be a problem if the best it can do is 4 or 5 pages at once. So we should insist on having 10 or 20 or 30 available pages. We can do our work in sections such as chapters, but for convenience we should be able to work with 30 pages or more continuously.

However, our RAM can only hold a part of these pages, and so our word processor must be able to read a portion of our text into RAM from the disk, allow us to work on it, and then move it back to the disk to make room for the next section we want. The word processor should do this without any intervention or attention from us, because we are busy writing and revising. Not all word processors behave this way, and if the one you are considering doesn't, look for another one.

Fourth, our word processor should be versatile and flexible so that we can make it fit our style of writing and the style of printing that our audience expects. If I do foreign languages, I need to know that the word processor can handle accents and other special symbols. If I do math or science, I need to know whether the program has provisions for special characters such as Greek letters or mathematical symbols. If I do scholarly research, the word processor should be able to handle footnotes and superscripts for the footnote numbers. Not every word processor can do everything, but the best of them can do almost everything. If you have special needs, be sure your magic program will be able to produce the necessary results.

Fifth, every word processor must produce text that can be printed on a printer. Because there are as many different printers as computers, our word-processor will be capable of making most of them do what they are capable of doing. If your printer can **boldface** text, then the word processor should be able to make it do it. If your printer does <u>under-lining</u> then the program should do it. And it should do these things easily and conveniently.

> This is an example of justified text. Word-processors can usually provide justified text. This is accomplished by distributing spaces in between the words to make the right hand margin line up evenly. Some programs, with the right printer, will justify by adding micro-spaces in between the words, which provides a better look. This paragraph is done that way.

> This paragraph includes **boldfaced** and <u>under-lined</u> text. In addition it uses super and sub

scripts as in a chemical formula, H_2O, or a mathematical formula, $a^2 = b^2 + c^2$.

Other effects such as changing from 12 pitch to another pitch and back are possible.

Special effects such as strikeovers and accents can also be achieved. For example: José Gómez.

~~Or a line with strikeovers.~~

Sixth, the word processor should be easy to use. This is one of the more important features of any program. If you can't make sense out of the manual, if the commands for making the program work are complex and obscure, if the program does not always do what you expect it to do, then it will not be easy to use. Since you can get good programs that are reasonably easy to use, you shouldn't settle for less. If your friends or a sales representative can't show you how to make the word processor work easily, find another friend, another sales representative, or another word processor.

Every word processing program has a logic and structure. Some are more logical than others. Some suit one writing style more than another. Personal preferences are much more important than whether some computer type thinks one word processor is more powerful than another. Such individuals probably can't type anyway and wouldn't know if the program works for people who write.

If you have learned the things talked about in this book, and are therefore computer literate, you'll find most quality word processing programs easy to use, although they will take some practice. The biggest surprise most people get is the tremendous increase in typing speed provided by the machine. I don't know what does it, but the ability to backspace and correct a mistake without leaving a trace encourages reckless speed, which, because there is no fear of error, ends up producing fast typing with fewer errors. Also you can get the computer to catch the errors.

That brings up item seven. A good word processor will permit its words to be checked for spelling with another program known by the esoteric name of spelling checker. These programs typically have dictionaries of some 45,000 words. They read your text, with the help of the microcomputer, find the words that don't match the dictionary, and then ask you what you want to do about it. You can change the word, leave it alone, add it to the dictionary, replace the word with something else, or quit.

Some of these programs will also analyze your writing, tell you how many different words you use, and identify over-used words and phrases. Some of us can't stand the criticism, but it's available if you need it.

Item eight is a bit more complicated. Some word processing programs, in the effort to be very fancy and provide special features, do unusual things to the way the computer stores your text on the disk. This is ok if the only thing you ever do with the text is process it with that program. But if you want to use another program on the text, perhaps a spelling checker, a typesetter, or a text analysis program, it may not work. So the eighth item is to get a word processor that will either produce standard text files on the disk or that can be made to produce those files if you need them.

Nine, a good word processor to choose is one used by many people where you work. In all computer work, there is much to recommend a policy of trying to have something standard used by many people you know. Then when you don't understand something, or when something doesn't work correctly, there will be lots of experienced people to help who don't have to come from a harried or uninformed sales staff at a local computer store. If you are willing to be a pathbreaker, you don't need either the advice or this book.

Ten, word processors that allow you to incorporate the results of other programs' activities can be most useful. Suppose you have a program, an electronic spreadsheet for example, that provides you with elegant tables illustrating your infallible method for making money in gold speculations. As you write what will surely be a best selling treatise on the subject, you want to insert this table into the text. But if your word processor can't copy the table produced by the spreadsheet program from the disk into your text, you have to retype the whole table. That is totally unnecessary. Try to pick compatible word processors and spreadsheet programs.

These ten commandments for a useful word processor provide general guidelines until you are ready to ignore them. When you know I'm wrong about something, then you are computer literate and can make your own choices. Nothing about word processors makes any sense, however, unless you actually try one. Don't let someone demonstrate it and then decide. You must make it work to know what it is like. And don't expect to make it do everything in the first ten minutes. You will need to enter and prepare at least ten or twenty pages of text before you can begin to know whether you like a word processor. Unless you have entered ten or twenty pages of text and printed it for your friends, you are not yet computer literate.

32

In addition to spelling checkers, most word processing programs provide assistance in what is called list processing. This is an arcane science that involves making a list, such as names and addresses, and then printing mailing labels.

List processing, to be precise, is doing something with a list. Now, you can do lots of complicated things with lists. You can have a list that has names, addresses, and salutations. The list processing option would allow you to prepare a form letter like the one below.

- - -

GOLD SPECULATIONS INC.
Bloomington, IN 47405

Dear ......,

I am pleased to send you the enclosed brochure on our latest gold bug speculation. If your money is burning a hole in your pocket, ..., please respond promptly so I can take it.

Sincerely yours,

Flybynight Alias
President

- - -

Then you tell the word processor and list processor to do their thing. The computer reads the form letter, asks the list processor for the heading and types something like:

- - -

GOLD SPECULATIONS INC.
Bloomington, IN 47405

Mr. Tom Jones
2234 Somewhere Street
Tomorrowland, USA

Dear Tommy,

I am pleased to send you the enclosed brochure on our latest gold bug speculation. If your money is burning a hole in your pocket, Tommy, please respond promptly so I can take it.

Sincerely yours,

Flybynight Alias
President

- - -

Having concluded with these two bits of unique information, the word processor gets a new page, and asks the list processor for the next heading:

Mr. Samuel J. J. Jones
1134 Nowhere Place
Yesterdaycity, USA

Asks for the salutation and types:

Dear Sam,

and then the form letter again.

There are many variations on this theme. Some list processing programs permit you to enter information at specific places in the form letter from the keyboard as the letter is printed. Other programs allow you to sort the list, select items from the list, and do other sophisticated things. Whether you need all this or not depends on the kind of work you do, but whatever word processing program you get should have this capability in some form.

Many publishers of books and articles, especially those interested in scholarly works, have found it useful to require manuscripts be delivered in machine readable form. A good word processing program should be flexible enough to produce machine readable copy in a format usable by the publisher. In these cases, the formatting of the text for publication may not be something that you do but rather something that the publisher does by inserting special printing codes into your text and then sending this text to a special typesetting machine to produce printed copy. In other cases, a publisher may ask for camera-ready copy. This means that you must provide the text formatted exactly as it will appear in the book. This book is an example of this style of publishing.

The great advantage of machine readable copy, and especially camera ready copy, is that much of the expense of publishing, the entering and correcting of text, is shifted to you, the author. While in the best of all possible worlds authors shouldn't have to enter their own text, in this world we often have to cooperate if we want our books to be sold at a reasonable price. This book would be twice as expensive if the publisher had to have it typeset.

If you anticipate publication of your work in camera ready form or a requirement for machine readable copy, be sure you find a word processing program that can deliver your text the way you and your publisher would like to see it. In general, if you expect to deliver machine readable text, any text editor will do fine, especially if it produces standard text files. For camera ready copy, you must have a word processing program whose formatting capabilities are adequate to produce a reasonably professional book.

Finally, there are a host of support programs for word processing that will prepare indexes, handle footnotes at the bottom of the page, add up columns of numbers in the text, and do other helpful things. Some word processing programs include these features in the main program, but most require separate programs to accomplish such specialized tasks. It is difficult to know whether these features are necessary, and especially to tell whether a particular support program will be adequate, until after you have some experience with word processing.

Because word processing is a universal application for computing, every programmer wants to write one. The result is a glut of programs that promise to solve every word processing problem. Several general principles can help guide you though the resulting thicket of overblown advertising claims.

First, consider the advertisements as mere suggestions of what the programmer's mother might say about the program, not as an indication of capability.

Second, never buy a word processing program you haven't had an opportunity to try, or can't return for a full refund.

Third, never buy a word processing program that has only been available for six months or less. It is almost certain to have bugs that will have to be removed. Let someone else test it, unless you get paid for it.

Fourth, buy a program that the rest of your colleagues use and recommend. It may not be the very best, but it probably works well and there will be lots of advice and assistance as you learn to use it.

Fifth, select word processing programs that fit well with your style of writing and that can accept information from companion programs that handle numbers and graphics.

Sixth, if you have special requirements such as foreign language alphabets, mathematical symbols, multiple fonts, complex text formatting needs, ignore all other advice and buy the program that accomplishes your tasks. In this case, invent the most difficult text you can imagine, take it to your friendly computer store, and ask them to show you how they would enter and print it. If they can't do it, you will have trouble.

Seventh, when considering any program and especially word processing systems, always ask about the maximums. What is the largest document the word processor can handle? How much disk space is required to handle that document? What other limitations does the word processor have? Often salespeople will not know the answers, and usually the advertisements do not dwell on limitations. However, if you read the error messages listed at the back of the word processor's manual you can frequently get a good idea of the limitations.

Eighth, as you try out various programs, be sure you enter a significant amount of text. Most word processors work fine for letters or short memos, but many are not adequate for 15, 20, or 40 page documents. Some become very slow, others get confused when they have to handle that much information.

If you follow all this advice, you will probably get a good, functional word processor. If you don't have the time or resources to do everything right, then simply buy the program that is most prevalent where you work, has been around for quite a while, and is a best seller. This may not put you on the cutting edge of technology, but it will give you a good, functional word processor with most of the bugs removed.

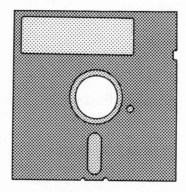

Floppy Disc

IV   Spreadsheet Calculators

Everyone with a microcomputer wants to do something with numbers. Indeed, these marvelous machines handle numbers with great speed and efficiency, and it would be foolish to have such power without the ability to use it. Of course, you can program the machine yourself to do a wide range of calculations. But that is tedious, and following one of the maxims of this book, it is always better to use a ready-made program to solve your computer problems.

The most flexible program for manipulating numbers is the spreadsheet calculator. Page after page of advertising tout the wonderful features of this Calc and that Calc; in fact these programs are wonderful.

A Calc program is conceptually a very simple thing. Imagine a sheet of paper divided into many boxes. Each box on the paper can hold a number or a label or a heading or a formula. You can arrange these items on the page in practically any way to produce a table, a record of transactions, a model of a process, or a series of calculations. Anything that can be done with a piece of paper divided into rows and columns can be done with the Calc, but of course with the Calc your mistakes are easily and instantaneously corrected.

- - -

	A	B	C	D	E	F	G	H
1	Price	_X_	Qty._	_=_	Cost_	_____	Part_	_____
2	20.00	_____	_3_	_____	60.00	_____	2001_	_____
3	15.00	_____	_4_	_____	60.00	_____	2002_	_____
4	30.00	_____	_1_	_____	30.00	_____	2003_	_____
5		_____	_____	_____	_____	_____	_____	_____
6	_____	Total	_____	_____	150.00	_____	_____	_____

- - -

If the numbers in column A, for example, and those in column C should be multiplied together to get the numbers in column E, the Calc program will do that for you. But even better, if you change your mind about the numbers in columns A or C, and modify them, the Calc will recalculate the numbers in column E instantaneously.

With this facility, the Calc can be set up with complex relationships between the numbers at one place on the sheet and those at various other places on the sheet. You can create amortization tables, for example, that will change according to the interest rate, the principal amount, or the payment.

Even more impressive, this sheet, created with the Calc program, can be rearranged, columns moved, rows added, labels and headings modified, and relationships changed with the simplest of commands. These changes rarely require that the rest of the sheet be changed. Only those things you want to change need be changed, everything else is automatically made to work with the new arrangement.

Obviously, this is a marvelous tool for accomplishing general purpose calculations. It can handle family budgets, loans, mortgages, or student grades. Its extreme flexibility and its relatively simple commands and rules make this program one of the most accessible computer applications available. Most people have no difficulty making the Calc programs work well, hence their tremendous popularity.

With the great range of Calc look-alikes available, choosing one can be more of a challenge than using one. However, the rules developed for selecting word processors can be helpful here.

First, buy a Calc that has been on the market for at least six months, that most of your co-workers use, and that produces output your word processor will accept.

Second, ask your computer store to demonstrate how the Calc works and how Calc tables can be incorporated into your word processor. If they can't do it, find another store or another Calc.

Third, find out how much memory is required for the Calc to work efficiently as a minimum and how much can be handled as a maximum. If your computer has too little memory or too much memory, find another Calc.

Fourth, if you like graphics, ask what kind of relationship exists between the Calc and programs that produce pie charts, bar charts, line graphs, and the like. When the sales people say it is easy, ask them to show you. If they can't do it easily, find another store or another Calc.

Having said such good things about the Calcs, let me also indicate some of their limitations. These programs are general purpose tools. As a result they are never as efficient or as capable as special purpose tools. Thus, if you need lots and lots of amortization tables, for example, a special purpose program that generates them will probably work faster and better than the Calc. If you only want to keep track of your checks, a checkbook program will do it more efficiently than a Calc. Similarly, a gradebook program will do grades easier too. But if you want tc do all of these, and if you often have lots of different small tables to prepare, each with different characteristics, there is no better program than the Calc.

Calcs also fail when the task is very complex or very large. While some Calcs will handle large sheets with many rows and columns, when the job gets complex and the amount of data involved is substantial, you will probably be better served by a more sophisticated program. The Calcs work best on problems that can be envisioned in terms of one or a sequence of tables that each would fit on one piece of graph paper. You can exceed that by about two or three times, but larger problems require more specialized solutions.

All the Calcs can print their results on a printer, or save the table to disk. However, not all the Calcs keep the data in a form that can be used by other programs. If you think you may want to use the data from another program or transfer data to another program, ask the sales people to show you how it is done with their Calc.

42

V   Communications

Once you have your microcomputer and have made it
do many of the wonderful things that make these
machines such fine tools, you are likely to become
interested in learning how your computer can communicate with the rest of the world. Practically all
microcomputers can be made to work as terminals to
talk to other computers, either micros or large
computers at universities or commercial concerns.

Communications technology is still very much in a
state of rapid change. There are many ways of
making computers talk to each other, and because
much money remains to be made in this business, the
various companies compete vigorously to prove that
their system should be the standard used by one and
all. If you have any interest in communications, a
few basic notions will help you begin.

Computers can be attached to each other in a
bewildering variety of ways. Usually, the process
works something like this. Imagine that an Apple
IIe and an IBM PC want to share some information.
The Apple has the information and the IBM needs it.
Because the Apple IIe and the IBM PC do not speak
the same internal language, we must put a translation device on each machine.

This translation device takes the Apple's data and
translates it into a form that the translator

attached to the IBM understands. Then the translator on the IBM converts this into a form compatible
with IBM internals. The nice thing about this is
that the code running between the two translators
follows a standard that can be understood by most
computers equipped with communications devices.
Thus, if we have the translation device, we can talk
not only between Apple IIes and IBM PCs, but also
between these microcomputers and any other machine
appropriately equipped.

Most microcomputers communicate in what is called
serial mode through a translation device called an
RS-232-C serial port. This jargon simply indicates
that RS-232-C is the name of the set of specifications that describes how the information will be
sent and how it will be received. If both computers
adhere to these specifications, the communication
will take place without problems.

The word serial indicates that the information
will be sent serially, one bit at a time, along
wires from one computer to another. The word port
means that this is accomplished through an opening
into the internal workings of the computer.

So what we have with an RS-232-C serial port is
the description of a way to move information back
and forth across wires connected between two computers. Most computers will have such a port as part
of their normal equipment because the port can also
be used to communicate with a letter quality printer
and a variety of other devices besides other computers.

Most microcomputers also have a parallel port
which has the same function as the serial port but
accomplishes it differently. Where the serial port
sends information one bit at a time, the parallel
port sends all eight bits at once and the receiving

44

device, usually a printer, must be prepared to accept all eight bits at once. A parallel port needs a cable with eight or more wires and is usually limited to very short distances of about ten feet.

While parallel communication is very fast, and easier to accomplish than serial communication, it is practical only for printers and other devices that can be located close to the computer. Moreover, while most microcomputers implement the parallel port in much the same way, there is no standard equivalent to the RS-232-C. On most microcomputers, the parallel port is included for the purpose of connecting a dot matrix printer.

Now, that seems easy enough, but what if the computer we want to talk to is several blocks or miles away? Clearly we don't want to string wires all over the place just to talk to a number of different computers. The answer, of course, is to use the phone. Unfortunately, the phone line cannot be simply plugged into a serial port at each end.

Instead, another device is required. This one translates computer talk from RS-232-C into telephone talk at Computer-1 and sends it out over the phone line to a similar device that translates telephone talk back into RS-232-C at Computer-2. This device is called a modem. For those interested in the origins of jargon, a modem is a contraction of Modulator-Demodulator which describes the essential technical function of the modem.

In choosing communications hardware such as modems, the options are many. Modems come in all shapes and sizes and prices. The differences can be irrelevant or significant depending on what kind of communications you want to do. If, for example, you would like to be able to call up the Dow Jones Company service that sends data on stocks and other

financial information to subscribers, you will need
to get a modem that is compatible with what the Dow
Jones computer expects. Similarly, if you expect to
talk to a university computer system, you must be
able to dial in with a modem set up to speak to that
system.

Although the business is highly technical, most
microcomputer users can communicate with most computers of interest through an RS-232-C port and a 300
baud modem. Wait!, you say. What is this 300 baud
stuff? Ok, more necessary jargon.

Most modems are advertised in terms of how fast
they can send information and receive information
across the telephone. Most universities and commercial systems will accept data at the rate of 300
bits per second which is a speed commonly advertised
as 300 baud. Many systems will also receive and
send at 1200 bps or 1200 baud. The advantage of the
faster speed is smaller telephone charges if you
have to call long distance, and shorter connect time
if you have to pay a connect time charge. However,
the 1200 baud modem costs about 4 times as much as
the 300 baud modem, so you may not need that much
speed.

Modems also come with many additional features,
all at a price, of course. Some will dial the phone
for you, some will answer the phone if another
computer calls you. Some have programs that allow
your microcomputer to pretend that it is a particular brand of computer terminal. All of these features can be useful if you need them.

Additionally, microcomputers require some kind of
program to make the process of communicating with
another computer convenient and efficient. These
programs turn the microcomputer into a terminal
connected to the host computer, and they allow you

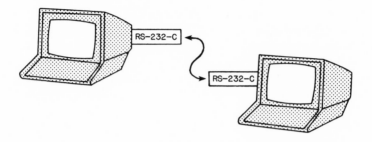

Local Communications

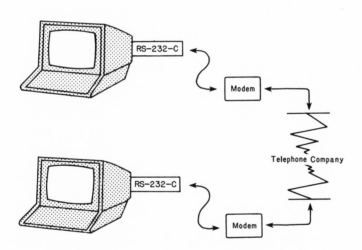

Long Distance Communications

to operate the host as if you were a standard terminal. They handle the housekeeping of switching from
being a not very smart terminal talking to another
computer to being a microcomputer that wants to do
something with the information sent or received from
the other computer.

Such programs come with a bewildering variety of
features, and they are usually designed for a specific microcomputer. Purchasing such a program requires that you seek advice from the operators of
the other computer or computer system to be sure
that what you buy will work with the other system.
In every case, you must try the combination of RS-
232-C, modem, and communications program before you
agree to buy. Otherwise you run a high risk of
unhappiness and frustration.

Much of the frustration in microcomputer communication comes from conflicts over handshaking protocols. Computer types, although not always friendly
themselves, recognize that the machines they design
need to behave politely to each other so that communication can be facilitated. Handshaking refers to
the etiquette followed by the various devices in the
course of a conversation between them. This etiquette permits a computer and a printer, for
example, to communicate across an RS-232-C line even
though the printer cannot accept data as fast as the
computer is sending it. Hence the two devices need
to agree on the handshaking protocol.

This protocol consists of signals that the sending
device and the receiving device agree to exchange to
indicate when the receiving device needs time to
catch up with the data already sent by the sending
device. So when the receiver sends the signal that
says "wait a minute," the sender stops until the
receiver sends the signal that says "ok, send some
more data." Such a handshaking protocol is essen-

tial both between printers and computers and between two computers, because it almost never happens that both devices operate at exactly the same speed.

Unfortunately, there are many types of handshaking protocols, and unless both machines agree, communication can be garbled or lost completely. Most communications programs allow you to select what kind of handshaking the receiving computer needs, but be sure to test it by sending and receiving a relatively long file of perhaps 20 pages of text. If the handshaking is wrong, the text will be missing characters or the communications will fail completely. The same test can be used to test computer-to-printer handshaking.

Why, you are asking by now, would I want to bother with all this? Well, of course, you may not want to bother. But here are some of the things that microcomputer users do with their communications capabilities.

Every university has a computer center, usually equipped with one or more relatively high-powered computers and software programs. If your work requires the manipulation of large amounts of data or statistical analysis of any complexity, there may be occasions when you need the power and sophistication available on larger machines that are not yet available on your microcomputer.

If you have communications capabilities in your microcomputer, you can use the university's big machine for those tasks that require it. You can collect and prepare your data on the microcomputer, and then, when you have everything ready, you can call up the big machine, transfer your data to it, ask for the complicated analysis, and when it is done, transfer the results back to the microcomputer for further work.

Many academics require large data files that are impractical to keep on microcomputer disks, but they work with much smaller subsets of these large files for their daily work. If equipped with the appropriate communications equipment, a microcomputer can be used to extract the required small subset of data, download it to the microcomputer and do the necessary analysis. Moreover, microcomputers can be used as data entry stations, collecting data in manageable sets and then uploading them to the main computer at convenient intervals. Because access to university main computers is often restricted, difficult, or limited in time, the freedom offered by the microcomputer to main frame connection can greatly improve academic productivity.

Some scientific fields, especially physics, require the specialized services of unique computing machinery, usually located in some far-away spot. Although it is possible to access these machines with a modem and a dumb terminal, many scientists find a microcomputer much more useful in preparing work for the big machine and retrieving results.

Many private information utilities exist around the country. These are nothing more than large computers that maintain big data files on a wide variety of topics. Some of them, such as the Dow Jones, specialize in one kind of information, in this case financial data and stock and bond reports. Some offer special services to the academic community such as bibliographic searches. Others, such as The Source, try to be more general in their interests with news, information on computers, programming languages, bulletin boards, financial information, and other data available to anyone who has signed up.

You get access to these information utilities by subscribing. You pay a subscription fee that entitles you to dial up the machine and use whatever resources are available. Of course, you have to pay for the phone bill and there is often a connect charge that bills you for the number of minutes you are connected to the other computer.

In addition to these formal resources, there are many informal dial-up systems. Most of are hobbyist bulletin boards. These are nothing more complicated than somebody with a microcomputer, a telephone number, and a communications device. If you know the number, you can call them up, and for the price of the phone call you can browse through the public bulletin board where other callers have left messages for the world to read. In addition, most of these hobbyist bulletin boards support some kind of electronic mail. This simply allows you to leave a private message for a particular person or receive a private message. These bulletin boards are often quite a lot of fun to read, although the quality of discourse in the public section can descend to rather low levels. Every part of the country has these home-grown bulletin boards, so it is rarely necessary to use a long distance call.

It is also possible for microcomputers to be hooked together, either to operate as a network or to share some resources such as a large storage device or a special purpose printer. If the distance between the machines is short, the equipment required to hook several machines together is not particularly complex or expensive, but the techniques for doing so go beyond the needs of literacy and trespass into the domain of computer expertise.

Electronic mail, another trendy phenomenon of the computer society, also requires communications equipment and programs. The principle of electronic mail is deceptively simple. You call up a network, you leave a message addressed to me. I call up the

network and check my mailbox to see if there are any
messages. I find the one you left me. I read it
and then I answer it by leaving a message addressed
to you. And so it goes. However, for all this to
work, I need a computer that can talk to your computer and vice versa. In addition, we both need some
place to leave the mail. So usually, we agree to
use a third computer as the mail drop. This third
computer is likely to have a large memory to handle
all the messages left by me, you, and the rest of
the people who participate in this mail network.

Getting everyone to agree on what we will do and
how we will do it is not as easy as it might seem,
but gradually some electronic mail networks do
appear. Often they occur within a company or a
university or some professional association. There
is an in-house network with electronic mail. Then,
I find out about it and even though I live in
another city I ask to participate in the net because
I need to exchange information rapidly with some of
the people who work at the central office. They say
ok and give me a phone number; I make sure my computer can talk to their computer and start using the
net. It is such fun and so effective that others
want to join too, and soon we have reasonably efficient electronic mail. But of course our little
system is most likely incompatible with similar
systems set up at other places, and so a generalized
network is still some distance away.

Corporations and universities generally have
highly developed, very sophisticated computer networks for their members to share specialized
computing resources and to move data and sometimes
electronic mail at high speed around their internal
system. If you belong to such an organization or
work with one frequently, it is essential to purchase communications equipment that can work at some
level with the internal system. Frequently it is

52

just as cheap and simple to buy the compatible programs and equipment as something else, but given the idiosyncrasies of computer communications networks, be sure to check first before believing any sales talk about total compatibility.

Given the growing importance of shared information and resources for computing, anyone claiming computer literacy needs to be conversant with the various dimensions of computer communications.

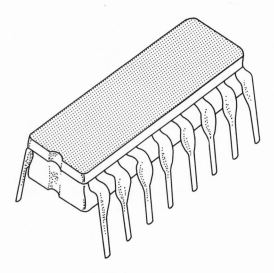

Computer Chip

VI Computer Languages

For all the technological wizardry that may be
contained in the hardware of your microcomputer, the
potential will remain unrealized without software
programs to make the equipment do something useful.
Word processing, spreadsheets (Calcs), and communications programs are examples of complex software
applications that make the machinery do useful
things. Each of these applications requires a program to tell the computer what to do and how to do
it.

While the computer literate user need not have
professional programming skills to make use of this
machine, some knowledge of what programming is and
how it is done can help you make intelligent decisions about computing and computing solutions.

Like everything else in the computer business,
programming comes in an incredibly broad variety of
non-standard formats. While there are general families and categories of programming and programming
languages, there is practically no standardization
at all in the implementation of programming tasks.

The key to programming, of course, is the process
itself, which is relatively easy to describe if not
so easy to do. Programming involves the preparation
of a set of instructions that tell the computer what
needs to be done and how to do it. In addition to

54

this primary task, the program also has to manage all the resources the computer will need to do the task. Let us take a very simple-minded example.

Suppose we want the computer to be able to add up two numbers and give us the result. Moreover, we want the computer to ask us what those numbers are, receive them from the keyboard, and print the result on the screen. The outline for such a program might look like this:

- - -

Addition Program Outline

Clear the screen to blank
Print a title "Addition Program"
Print five blank lines
Print a request for the first number
    "Please enter the first number."
Wait for the number to be typed on the keyboard
Store that number at storage place 1
Print a request for the second number
    "Please enter the second number."
Wait for the number to be typed on the keyboard
Store that number at storage place 2
Add the number at storage place 1
    to the number at storage place 2
Store the result at storage place 3
Print 5 blank lines
Print the message "First Number "
Get the number from place 1
    and print it on the screen
Print the message "Second Number "
Get the number from place 2
    and print it on the screen
Print a solid line under the two numbers
Print the message "Total"
Get the number from place 3
    and print it on the screen

```
Print 5 blank lines
Print the message
    "Add two more numbers (y/n)?"
Wait for a "y" or an "n"
    to be typed from the keyboard
If it is a "y" go to the top of this program
    and do it again
If it is an "n" print the message "End"
End the program
```

- - -

As you can see, because the computer is not very smart, it takes quite a lot of instructions to tell it to do relatively simple things. However, because much of what the computer does is not unique to this program or any other program--getting information from the keyboard, printing it on the screen, storing things into memory, recalling them from memory, and the like--various computer languages have been developed that make preparing instructions for the machine easier by having ready made instruction sequences.

The many available computer languages differ one from the other in a variety of dimensions. Some languages try to allow the programmer easy access to the way the machine stores its information and manages its hardware resources. Those languages usually allow the programmer to write fast and efficient programs, but at the cost of having to pay very close attention to the hardware characteristics of the computer.

Other languages sacrifice some of this efficiency and speed in order to make the programmer's task of specifying the solution to the problem at hand easier. These languages tend to be somewhat slower and less efficient, but easier to learn and use. Moreover, the programs written for these languages

56

often, but not always, can more easily be revised to work on a different brand of computer.

Because people write programs to accomplish widely differing tasks, it comes as no surprise to discover that no programming language provides the optimal solution to every problem. Some languages do wonders with financial applications, some handle words and letters easily, while others work especially well with scientific problems. Some handle small jobs quickly, while others are more efficient with large problems. Some languages teach good programming habits, making programs that are easy to revise and improve. Other languages, while fast and efficient, produce programs that only the original programmer can understand, revise, or improve.

High level microcomputer languages, to over-simplify a bit, come in two main varieties: interpreted and compiled. These two jargon words indicate how the computer goes about reading the program you write and turning it into something it understands.

Computers, of course, can only understand instructions presented to them as a sequence of ones and zeros. We, however, don't think that way. So practically all programs are written in something that looks almost intelligible to humans, whether words, symbols, letters, or formulas. However, the computer must take this program we understand and translate it into the ones and zeros it understands. This translation can take place in one of two major ways.

Interpreted programs work like this. You write a program, a sequence of instructions. Then you tell the computer to run the program. The computer reads your first instruction, interprets it by turning it into the appropriate ones and zeros, and then executes the first instruction. It then takes the second instruction, and does the same thing. It does this until it gets to the end or until there is an error in the program. When it is done, you have the result or the error message and your program can be fixed, if it is wrong, or saved, if it worked.

When you want this program to do its thing again, the computer repeats this interpretation sequence each time. One of the benefits of this process is that it is very easy to test your program as you prepare it, because you can ask the computer to try out your instructions any time you want without any intermediate steps. Of course, the disadvantage is that the computer must interpret each instruction into its ones and zeros every time it runs the program. As a result, interpreted languages tend, all things being equal, to be slower than what are called compiled languages.

A compiled program works this way. You write the program, same as you did for the interpreted language. But before the computer can try it out, you first run it through a compiler program. The compiler takes your sequence of instructions and translates them into the appropriate ones and zeros for the computer. When the compiler gets done, it prepares another program made up of the ones and zeros. Thus, you now have two versions of the original program--the one you can read and the one the computer can read.

You then run the compiled program. The computer, if it likes it, will do what you asked it to do quickly and efficiently. You then save both versions of the program and you're done. But if there are errors in the original program, and there are always errors, you must correct them in the original, run the original through the compiler, and then ask the computer to try again. Thus, there are more steps and more complications in using compiled languages than in using interpreted languages.

These characteristics help explain the universal popularity of the Basic language on microcomputers. In most microcomputers, Basic is an interpreted language (although it is possible to have compiled Basic as well). Because the language is relatively simple, is easily understood by people not very experienced with computing, and allows you to generate simple programs rapidly and efficiently, most microcomputer users find Basic a congenial computing language. However, as most computer scientists will tell you, Basic is inelegant, teaches bad programming habits, is slow, and should be replaced by any one of a number of languages. All of this, while true, is for many of us beside the point.

Unless you are going to be a professional programmer, there is little advantage to a more efficient language. Basic is an ideal programming language for short, quick, home-grown programs. If you have a long and complex operation, you are usually better off buying a ready-made package than trying to develop the program yourself. If there is no ready-made package, then you should try to find a professional programmer to help you identify a better solution.

In the microcomputer world, three varieties of programming languages have received the most attention. First, of course, is Basic. This language comes in many dialects, all of them sharing a general structure and a more or less common vocabulary. However, each microcomputer Basic has special features and commands that refer to that machine's unique features. This is especially so for graphics capabilities which are very dependent on the brand and model of microcomputer involved. As a result, while Basic programs look very much alike, only the most trivial program written on one machine will run reliably on another machine. At the same time, people who can program skillfully in Basic on one machine can usually transfer that skill with no difficulty to another microcomputer.

The second most popular language is Pascal. Pascal is an elegant programming language that teaches good programming habits. It is, however, a compiled language in the sense outlined above. While there are many varieties of Pascal, the version called UCSD Pascal is likely to become something of a standard. This provides a much greater degree of uniformity than is available with Basics, and for professional programmers, this ability to transport a program from one microcomputer to another is a major advantage. If you are interested in programming for its own sake, moreover, you will probably want to learn Pascal as well as Basic. Computer science professionals think that you learn to be a better programmer if you start with Pascal rather than Basic.

However, for computer literacy, you really don't have to know any computer languages.

In addition to high level languages such as Basic and Pascal, microcomputers are frequently programmed in either what is called Assembly language or what is known as an applications language. These two varieties are at opposite ends of the spectrum. Assembly language is very close to the ones and zeros and provides the programmer with very precise control over the hardware resources of the machine. The applications languages, in contrast, are far removed from the machinery, focusing instead on the application.

Applications languages are most often implemented

to solve two kinds of problems. The first are statistical manipulations of large data sets. A package of statistical routines linked together with a data preparation program constitute an application language. You prepare a set of instructions in the application language and the program then prompts you to enter data, asks you what you want done with the data, does the statistical analysis, and returns a report of the results. You need not be concerned about the details of the process at all, since the applications language takes care of all that for you. Of course, what you gain in ease of use you frequently lose in flexibility. The program will prepare your results in a more or less standard format, whether you think it elegant or not. Nonetheless, these applications languages are easy to use, and while programming experience helps make sense out of the instructions, it is rarely necessary.

The second major applications language category involves data base or file management programs. These are complex sets of routines that make it easy to invent a collection of data, input the data, store the data, revise it, manipulate it by combining, sorting, analyzing, and print it back out with a complex set of selection or formatting requirements. These programs are called data base managers or file managers and the details of their design and operation are very complex. Fortunately, you don't need to know much about these internals, only whether the program will do what you want with your information and do it easily. The only way to evaluate such a program is to try it out on a representative sample of your information and read the fine print about any limitations the program may have.

Finally, there is a category of applications called integrated systems. These come in many forms

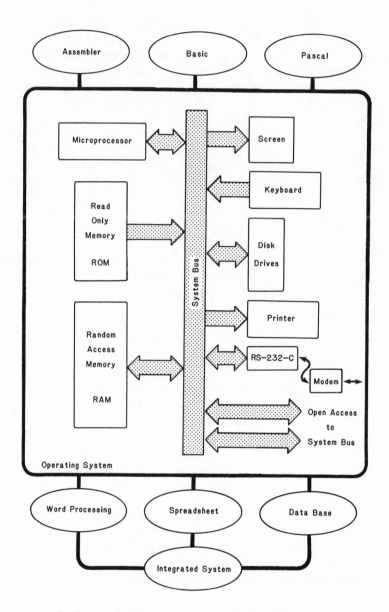

A Complete Microcomputer System

and provide unlimited opportunity for advertising exaggeration and hyperbole. An integrated system is nothing more complicated than a combination of applications programs that are packaged in such a way that you can move from one program to another without complications.

For example, you could have a word processor, a Calc, and a graphics program bundled together so that in the middle of writing a report you could push a key and do some spreadsheet calculations, and then prepare a graph using the spreadsheet results. At the conclusion of this routine, you would return to the report with the Calc table and the graph inserted into the prose text of your report. Nifty.

Some integrated systems also combine the operating system and these applications into a total system that uses common commands and rules for operation. These integrated systems are possible because more and more of the new microcomputers have large memories of 256K or more and large disk storage capacities. Thus it is possible to have lots of program and data in memory at one time.

The disadvantages of these integrated systems are several. Frequently you find that while you like the Calc and the graphics program you can't tolerate the word processor. If that's the case, you're stuck because it is difficult or impossible to undo the package and replace the offending program.

If the integrated system includes the operating system, it is likely to be very difficult to include programs not prepared by the manufacturer of the integrated system.

Given the complexity of these systems, and the likelihood that they will change rapidly over the next few years, my advice is to approach anything claiming a total solution with extreme caution. This is especially so if the integrated system uses special codes or prepares data files in a non-standard format. Remember, if it hasn't been on the market and in the hands of users for at least six months and if it isn't in its second revision at least, don't trust it unless you like to experiment and can tolerate significant frustration.

Programming, then, is a complex and sophisticated discipline. It is lots of fun to do as an amateur, but never suppose that the implementation of a complex process will be easily accomplished. Programming requires much skill, and the computer world is full of people who are very good at writing programs that are 90% correct. Unfortunately, that missing 10% usually proves to be critical for your needs. Approach custom programming with great suspicion and care. If you get a good programmer who will stick with you until the job is done right, you will get a fine result. That doesn't always happen, so be sure to request references before hiring a professional programmer, and call the references.

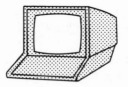

Computer Terminal

VII   How to Buy a Personal Computer

Now that you are computer literate, you need a computer, for what good is literacy without its object?   Even the most cursory glance at a microcomputer magazine will show a bewildering variety of machines available, each with the most wonderful of features and persuasive of advertisements.   All of your friends will offer good advice based almost exclusively on what computer they own, and they will regard you as extremely foolish if you don't get the same machine they have.   Your friendly computer retailer will tell you that the super duper machine in his window is the very best, but when you return next week and there is another machine in the window, you will hear that this new one is surely the best for all time.

Fortunately, the first rule of the microcomputer business is that whatever hardware you buy will be obsolete next week.   Thus, you need be less concerned that you have the best and most wonderful machine in the world because even if you do, it won't stay that way long enough for you to figure out how to make it work.

With this sense of reality, it becomes easier to separate out what you should look for in a microcomputer. The following should provide you with some guidance in this search.

65

First, try to decide what you want the machine to do. Many people pursue technological sophistication without much thought about the purpose of all this computing power. If you want a special purpose machine to manage a small business or assist with scientific experiments, then you can write down all the things the machine will need to do and proceed with your search. If your requirements are more generalized, that is if you want a machine for the kids, one that will do your taxes and handle your correspondence and teach you programming, then you will have a harder time separating the winners from the losers.

Next, figure out how much you want to spend. You can spend lots and lots of money on microcomputers. Never believe an advertised price until you know what else you have to buy to make the machine do what you need it to do. The price range you select will narrow the range of options.

The third guideline is to find out what the people at your business, university, or elementary and high schools are using. Decide whether you want to have company as you work with your machine or whether you have the time and resources to be a lone ranger. This too can help you narrow the range of possible machines.

Fourth, discover what software programs you think you want for word processing, for games, for education, for scientific uses. Not all programs are available for all machines. Some programs require color displays, some require graphics, some need large memories. Whatever specificity you can establish here will further narrow the range of possible machines.

Fifth, decide how long you will have to live with this machine, knowing that better and cheaper ma-

66

chines will surely be available within three years or less. If you expect to keep the machine a long time (in this business that is about five years or more), you want to buy from a big company that will support the machine even after it has become technologically obsolete. It may be worth a few dollars more to have the large corporation behind your equipment if you can't trade up every three or four years.

The sixth recommendation is to identify the service capabilities of the computer stores in your area. How will you get the disk drives fixed? How long will it take to have the computer diagnosed and fixed? What will it cost? What happens when your computer retailer goes out of business?

Then, decide to what extent you want this machine to be expandable. In almost every case, the ability to attach new gadgets to the machine will raise its price, but at the same time this ability may protect you against premature obsolescence since the gadgets may convert your machine to take the next advance in technology. The more general your uses for the machine, the more likely you will want to change, add, or modify what your machine can do as you acquire experience and sophistication.

Finally, choose an operating system. Operating systems help determine what software can run on your machine and how interchangeable programs and data will be between your micro and other micros. CP/M, CP/M-86, and MS-DOS are currently the standard general operating systems. Any one of them gives considerable flexibility.

Apple DOS (for the Apple II, II+, and IIe) has the largest software base of the proprietary operating systems, but it is incompatible with the other operating systems. The UCSD P-system provides an operating system especially designed for a Pascal environment but capable of handling other programming languages. It has a large following, but not as large as the CP/M environment.

The various virtues and liabilities of operating systems are usually beyond the comprehension of all but the most expert of users, and the expert users often are most enthusiastic about the operating system they have or wish they had, rather than the most practical one. The best bet is to buy the operating system that will run the applications you know you need now, that has the largest software base, and is used by the most people you work with or know. Not a scientific way of evaluating operating systems, but it will work rather well for non-technical people.

After working your way through these steps, you will probably have narrowed your choice down to one or two machines. At this point, it probably doesn't make much difference which you get. Most microcomputers of about the same price and features will work about the same. The differences are usually so minor or invisible that unless your application is very specific and demanding, you won't be able to tell the difference. If you like the looks, feel, style, or name, that is probably as good a reason to make a choice at this point as any esoteric technical consideration.

Once you pick a machine, you usually have to make some decisions about how to package it, what accessories to buy and the like. Of course, if you have decided on a completely integrated package with no choices, then you are done. You take it home, plug it in, open the manual, and start having fun.

But if you have a general purpose microcomputer, you will probably have to make many decisions about

how to put it together, configure it in the jargon
of the trade. Usually this means you have to decide
how much memory, what kind of disk drives, and what
type of display or screen. You may also need to
learn about printer types and features to make a
choice.

Memory--Memory for computers is getting cheaper by
the day. A useful microcomputer can be put together
with 48K (about 48 thousand characters) of memory,
but anyone buying now should have a minimum of 64K,
and the computer should probably be able to accept
two times this much memory that you can add in later
as memory prices continue to decline.

Be sure to check to see if your word processing
program will work with only 64K, because often you
really need 128K to make it perform well. The rule
of thumb is that you will never have enough memory.
Parkinson's law holds; you will fill up whatever
memory you get within the first 6 months or less.

Disk Drives--Sometimes you have no choice here;
you get whatever the manufacturer installs. But if
there is a choice, two drives are generally better
than one.

The capacity of disk drives varies considerably
from manufacturer to manufacturer. Most microcomputer users find that 150K per drive is a rock bottom
minimum, and that twice that approaches comfort.
With disk drives as with memory, you never have
enough, but you can do pretty well with two 300K or
bigger disk drives. However, if you are antici-
pating activities that will use large files, text
with more than 150K of characters per document that
cannot be subdivided into sections for example, then
you will need more disk storage. That is because
many word processing programs require at least twice
and sometimes three times as much space available on

69

the disks as is in the document being processed.

Large business applications such as inventories or complex accounting may also take up lots of disk space. In these cases, you may need to investigate hard disk drives which start at about 5 megabytes (about 5 million characters) and go up to 10 or 20 megabytes.

Hard disk drives are very similar to the floppy disk drives except they will hold much more information because they use a rigid, usually nonremovable, disk for storage. These are expensive, but they provide very fast and large external storage. If you think you need one, get some good advice from your local university or other experts not selling hard disks.

Remember, however, that floppy disks of the 5-1/4" size most common on microcomputers are usually incompatible between machines. Thus, if you have an IBM and your friend has an Apple, you can't take data recorded on his disk and put it into your machine.

Displays--Some computers come with the screen as an integral part of the machine. But many allow you to purchase the screen as a separate component. The range of features in screens is large. You can get two kinds of color screen; you can get green or brown or amber or black-and-white monochrome screens. You can get them in 9", 13", or bigger sizes and in a variety of cabinets.

Cheap monitor screens can be very satisfactory if color graphics are not required. Also, you can usually sell a monitor easily if you want to get a better one. In any event, always see the monitor in action, attached to your machine, running your most important programs, before you buy. Individual taste and preference are very important since you spend such a lot of time looking at this screen. If you don't like the way it looks, try another screen.

Printers--You can currently get printers from about $500 to well over $2000. The cheapest printers that provide flexibility and reasonably good quality are dot matrix printers. You can get an incredible variety of features in these dot matrix printers, so you will need to decide how much fanciness is necessary. Always make your dealer hook up the printer and show you how it works. If you need letter quality, you will need a daisy wheel printer or its equivalent. These are usually more expensive and slower than dot matrix printers, but they do put out good looking copy. This book is printed on such a machine.

Here, as with all hardware, the technical differences between printers in much the same price range are not great, and you should buy a printer that has many local people using it, for which there are repair facilities, and that can print the type of documents you expect to produce. If you require lots of graphics, you will want a dot matrix printer. If you prepare manuscripts for publication, your editors may demand letter quality.

Once you have the hardware and the software, you are ready to begin computing. Never be afraid to ask anyone else what may be a dumb question. Some computer people try to make you feel stupid if you don't know your bits from your bytes, but don't be intimidated. It is their fault that you have to learn anything at all, for if the computer professionals did their job right, the instructions would be sufficient and the machines would work as described. When they don't and when the instructions are opaque, computer people should be grateful for the opportunity to help you out.

VIII How to Gain Computer Literacy

With the increased interest in microcomputers in colleges and universities, in the public schools, in business, and in the home, many people want to design or participate in courses or programs designed to achieve computer literacy. When they look for examples of successful courses, they find a multiplicity of models, some free-wheeling and permissive, some highly directed. They find short courses, medium courses, and long ones. The confusion here reflects, naturally, the many different ways organizations and people regard computer literacy.

There is no reason to despair, however, for the important thing about computer literacy is that you get it, not how you get it. Computer literacy is much like traditional literacy; even though you learned to read on novels, once you became literate you found little difficulty applying that ability to newspapers, poems, technical books, or whatever interested you. The key to traditional literacy is the ability to open the book and make sense out of the words on the page. Once you have mastered that skill, you can refine it by reading and studying poetry, or physics textbooks, or gourmet cookbooks.

Computer literacy works the same way. Once you learn how to operate a computer, you understand its basic functions and processes, and you can make it usefully do a number of tasks, it is then relatively easy to branch out on your own to acquire specialized computer skills appropriate to your interests, work, or amusement.

Any computer literacy course can help you toward this goal, but some computer literacy designs are more likely than others to be generally helpful.

Although there are as many definitions of computer literacy as there are people to define it, the following notions may help focus attention on the kind of skills and knowledge that might be included in a short course designed to teach computer literacy to adults.

Every computer literacy course for adults must teach the participants how to recognize problems for which the computer may be a useful part of the solution. This goal will be achieved by concentrating not on the problems themselves, for it is impossible to anticipate all of them, but on the capabilities and limitations of the microcomputer, and especially on the logic of its design and organization. If we understand the general principles that govern the operation and design of these machines, we can more easily identify ways in which this technology can help us solve particular problems.

Computer literate adults will be able to identify appropriate computer resources for a wide range of tasks and they will know how to ask a variety of experts for assistance in developing solutions using computers. Moreover, computer literate adults will have an understanding of problem design and problem solution appropriate for computer applications, a skill that can be acquired through acquaintance with computer languages or through the solution of common problems using other computing tools.

73

Because each profession or discipline has different specific needs that can be met by computers, it is impossible to develop a generic computer literacy course. The content of a series of sessions designed for elementary school teachers would not contain the same information as a course for college students majoring in chemistry. But all of these computer users need a minimum baseline of knowledge about the computer, and these minimum guidelines for computer literacy can be specified.

The minimum course in computer literacy would require about sixteen hours of carefully planned instruction. The course, if it is to be successful, must include not only readings such as this book, but also a substantial amount of experience at a real microcomputer, working with programs, with operating systems, files, data, and the like. Because computer literacy is like traditional literacy, you must do it for the instruction to be effective. Talking about computer literacy is fun, but it does not achieve literacy.

An ideal arrangement is a classroom with a computer for every participant, but certainly no more than two students per computer. More can be assigned to each machine, but at the cost of reducing the effectiveness of the instruction.

One of the more frequent errors in computer literacy classes is the tendency to teach about a particular computer as if knowledge of its special features were important to computer literacy. This is especially likely in courses designed by computer stores where one of the purposes of the class is to sell a particular brand of microcomputer. Computer literacy instructors must make every effort to stress the general principles, the transferable characteristics, and the universality of the concepts they teach. This can be done even while illustrating the particular implementation of a specific machine.

While the exact structure and content of this minimal computer literacy course will vary with the interests and knowledge of the audience, a university based course might be organized around the following four topics.

General Organization and Structure of Computers--Within the sixteen-hour limit on our hypothetical course, and assuming that every student will have read an introductory book, preferably this one, about two hours should be the minimum time devoted to this topic.

Although there are many ways to approach the organization and structure of computer equipment, the design of microcomputers offers some interesting advantages as a representative model of computer hardware. Many academics will acquire their first introduction to computing and the incentive to use computers through standard application packages implemented on small machines. Moreover, a general discussion of the principal features of small computers offers an accessible and relatively simple approach to the general functions of all computers, however actually implemented in hardware. A discussion of this topic should include, as a minimum, a clear understanding of the relationship of the principal functional parts of microcomputers.

Starting with the microprocessor, the course will discuss the basic operations of this central processing unit and how it interacts with both volatile random access memory (RAM) and permanent read only memory (ROM). The course must explain the bus structure of microcomputers with special emphasis on the role of this bus in linking the various parts of the machine to the microprocessor itself. This would include a discussion of the notions of bits, bytes, and the difference between 8-bit and 16-bit microcomputers. Such information is necessary for computer literates to cope with the advertisements and other literature related to small computers.

In addition to these central resources of microprocessor and memory, the computer literacy course must explain the functions and styles of keyboards, display screens, and printers as the most common, indeed virtually universal input-output devices, and show their relationship to the bus and through the bus to the main processor and the memory.

External storage, primarily disk drives, also deserves discussion, including a clear explanation of the differences between floppy disks and hard disks. This would include an explanation of the communications needed between disk, memory, and microprocessor carried out through the bus.

At the conclusion of this section, computer literates should have a clear understanding of the block diagram of microcomputers, although knowledge of the technical details of microcomputer architecture is probably unnecessary.

Information Organization--This section of computer literacy, which might also be allocated about two hours of the course, focuses on the movement and organization of data within the computer structure outlined above. It includes the notions of computer languages, operating systems, files, data, and the operation of software.

The discussion of computer languages should include an explanation of the microprocessor instruction set (that is the function of this machine language, not how to program it), the need for higher level languages to provide the instructions that make it possible for the main processor to accomplish useful work, and a very short discussion of common programming languages such as Basic or Pascal.

Operating systems can best be discussed in terms of what is available on the computers in the class, so that the role of the operating system in managing hardware resources and assisting in the management of software or programming tasks specified by the user can be demonstrated on a real machine. The instructor should give special attention to questions of operating system incompatibility and to a short survey of the strengths and weaknesses of some of the more prevalent microcomputer operating systems.

Because files and data constitute the raw material for computer work, the computer literate will need to understand the relationship of data to records to files in a general sense, as well as a clear notion of how data is collected (keyboard, disk file, real-time data acquisition), stored in memory or on disk or other medium, and processed. Emphasis should be placed on the relationship of the operating system in managing the data that is delivered to the main processor for manipulation in accord with the instructions provided by the programming language or applications package.

Software design is the last topic in this section. In emphasizing the function of software design in the solution of problems, this section should include an understanding of the logical progression of instructions from the level of machine language and assembly language, through the higher level languages such as Basic or Pascal, to the special purpose software packages such as dBase II or SPSS. Computer literates should understand the hierarchical nature of these software instruction sets,

77

and appreciate the trade-off between generality of function, ease of use, and specificity of purpose. It will be useful if everyone has the opportunity to learn enough of a language such as Basic to solve some simple problems.

   Problem Solving--Because the point of computer literacy is to improve the ability to solve problems, the computer literate individual will have experience with a number of relatively standardized computing tools. These tools are chosen not because they are necessarily the most useful for everyone, but because the problems they are designed to solve are of the most general nature and therefore illustrate many principles that will apply to the solution of more specialized problems. Because of the importance of this part of a computer literacy course, ten hours of the sixteen would be a reasonable minimum.

   Two activities are universally available on microcomputers: word processing and spreadsheet calculators.

   Word processing programs for microcomputers abound, and computer literates will find the use of any of these relatively easy. A course for computer literacy will include a full discussion of the organization and functions of word processing systems. The purpose of this discussion is not to teach any particular word processing system, but to identify and explain the things that need to be done in word processing and how particular programs can accomplish those functions. The focus will be on the functions of text entry, text editing, text formatting, and text storage. For this discussion to have any real effect, however, the participants in the course must have a real word processing program to use, they must enter text, edit text, and print text. Unless they can do this successfully,

78

they are not computer literate.

Spreadsheet programs exist in many forms and styles, but all of them accomplish virtually identical functions. While the previous example focused on the solution of problems specified in terms of text characters, this example emphasizes numerical solutions.

Because the spreadsheet is an easily understood concept, and because the problems that can be solved with such a tool are relatively straightforward, it is possible in a short time to demonstrate how to approach the solution of common numerical problems with such a tool. Here the emphasis will be on the design of solutions and how to implement the design on a particular spreadsheet program. No computer literate person should have difficulty making a spreadsheet program solve relatively simple problems in data display and analysis. But each participant must develop a sample spreadsheet problem and make the computer and program deliver a useful result.

Because the range of software applications is so large, some attention must be paid to other software solutions. Here there should be a discussion of the limitations of such tools as word processors and spreadsheets and a description of special purpose solutions. For example, academics always have a need for grade books. It is instructive to implement a grade book with a word processor, with a spreadsheet, and with a specially designed program. Such a demonstration will show clearly some of the differences between special purpose software and general purpose software. A similar example could be invented to demonstrate test construction.

Although the operation and design of data base systems is a complex topic, a course in computer literacy ought to touch on some of the more popular data base systems available for microcomputers and attempt to illustrate the differences between complex data base programs and less imposing but perhaps as useful file managers. Here, too, simple examples that can be implemented by the course participants will be very helpful.

University Resources--Because the microcomputer is but one computing resource available to academic faculty and staff, and often the one with the least computing power, the computer literate individual must have a clear understanding of the range of computing resources available at most colleges and universities. Given the limitations of time in a basic literacy course, this section, which would be on the order of two hours, can only skim the surface of the variety of topics outlined below. But computer literates, while they may not fully comprehend the detail of these topics, must have a clear understanding of the range of resources mentioned here.

This section should focus on such items as communications, time sharing, large scale package programs, data base management, specialized equipment, and technical assistance services.

Communications, while technically quite complicated, is relatively easy to explain and understand. Computer literates need to understand the differences between networks, time shared systems, and other common arrangements of computing equipment. In this section, there should be a strong emphasis on examples from an academic computing system to illustrate various configurations and functions. Communications includes not only data transfers, time sharing, batch processing, and interactive computing, but also an understanding of electronic mail, security, and information utilities.

Large scale applications package programs provide

another important dimension for academic computing. Most users experience big computers through these large scale packages. A general discussion of the nature of these major applications, and a clear discussion of their relationship to computing languages, operating systems, and data management, will greatly improve computer literacy. Computer literates should have had the experience of working with a simple example of a large statistical package such as SPSS and perhaps a large scale data base management package such as SIR. While basic literacy does not include the ability to implement complex solutions with these packages, it does include an understanding of their capability and availability.

Special equipment is often used with these large packages such as plotters, graphics terminals, and special printers. Computer literates should know what these devices can do and have an appreciation of how they can be made to function. They should also understand how the communications system described earlier operates to permit microcomputer based information and programs to use these special devices. The computer literate should not feel limited by the equipment in any one location but should understand the ability of networks to provide special purpose tools to anyone with access to the system.

Technical assistance is usually available within the academic environment, but it is not always clear what users should expect or how they should approach technical staff. Computer literates will know how to analyze their problem, have a clear idea of the kinds of solutions that may be available, and will be able to formulate appropriate questions for computer experts.

The key to the efficient use of technical

assistance is the ability to analyze problems and articulate precisely what information can be provided, what needs to be done to that information, and how it is to be presented when the analysis is completed. Often it is very helpful if computer literates have experience with programming languages or major large package programs in formulating their computing strategies. With such experience, you can contribute greatly to improvement and enhancement of technical services.

- - -

At the end of this intensive program, most participants will be approaching computer literacy. Of course, some fraction of this material can be learned in less time, and a more thorough treatment can be achieved with more time.

But computer literacy at this basic level is not enough to make you an efficient and effective computer user. That requires several additional things.

First, you need a microcomputer. Without access to a machine, all this talk about operating systems, program packages, and the like, comes to nothing. So the first priority for any organization that wants computer literates is to find a way to help its members get microcomputers. This can take the form of simply purchasing them outright and giving them to people, a not very efficient way to spread the word, to some form of subsidized purchase plan.

Organizations such as universities and colleges have many good reasons for assisting faculty and students in the purchase of microcomputing equipment. Since each individual will have to pay for some of the cost of the equipment, people who have no interest and no use for a computer will not get one. Because the machines will belong to the purchaser and not the institution, responsibility for security and care will devolve on those who use the machines, which are thus likely to get better care and closer attention.

If the organization subsidizes a particular brand of microcomputer, either through a cash discount or group purchase plans, the organization can have a significant influence on the number of different machines that are used within the organization. The fewer different machines, the easier communications, programming, and maintenance will be, given the great incompatibility that exists in the microcomputer business.

In short, the very first thing required for functional computer literacy is the computer, and unless you have one, the rest of the exercise is a waste of time.

Once you have a machine, you will find ways to use it and you will want to develop skill more closely focused on your own professional specialty. If you do words, you'll want to learn about editors, formatters, spellers, indexers, and the like. If you do numbers, you'll want to know about array processors, data bases, number crunching routines, and similar esoterica.

This information comes best from other people in your field who know about microcomputers. It also comes from magazines focused on microcomputer topics, especially from the advertisements in those magazines for products and programs useful in your discipline. The number of these magazines is large and increasing rapidly every day. There are journals devoted to particular brands of microcomputers (Apple, TRS-80, or IBM), and some devoted to special topics within a particular brand of microcomputer. Some are general purpose dedicated to hardware, others dedicated to software. You should browse through these and subscribe to at least one general purpose magazine and one devoted to your microcomputer.

Computer clubs also exist at most universities and in most communities. These, like the magazines, tend to be machine specific, and oriented toward special interests. They are primarily useful as places to exchange information on troubles and new products, and they often offer a way to discover who in your community knows a lot about what you need to know.

The commercial and free telephone bulletin boards and information utilities all have information exchanges that provide advice and counsel on hardware and software problems and evaluations. Sometimes they can be very useful, although the time invested in working with these services can be substantial.

How much of these resources you need depends a great deal on what you do with your microcomputer. If you have narrow, specialized requirements, you will find it easier to get information than if you have general purpose requirements that change. Because microcomputing is such a large and diverse field that changes so rapidly, few people, even the experts, can hope to stay current and have the answers to all kinds of problems. Often the best advice you can get comes not from some technical wizard, but instead from a user who has had the same problem you now have and found a solution. While this person may not know all the technical details underlying the solution, for most purposes, all you need is the solution.

Finally there are the books. Everyone, it seems, writes a book about microcomputing. There are hundreds of books on Basic programming, almost that many on Pascal. There are books focused on IBM, on Apple, on Pet, on Radio Shack computers. There are treatises on games, on data bases, on communications. Some books are very technical, some very elementary. You should get a few. But expect a new generation of books about every six months. These books help best when you have a particular interest, say learning how to program in Basic. You can get a good book on Basic, for example, preferably one that illustrates Basic as used on your microcomputer, and learn quite a bit about how to make the machine do what you want.

Whatever your use for the machine or your level of interest in microcomputing in general, the most important advice anyone can give you is to use the machine. Don't worry about making mistakes for you will make them and everyone makes them; don't worry about appearing foolish because any problems you have we all have had; and do try anything that you think might work. If it doesn't, nothing is lost and if it does, you've learned something new. Above all, never hesitate to ask questions, and when the answers don't make sense, ask again, ask someone else. Eventually you'll find someone who actually knows the answer and can explain, or you'll figure it out yourself.

Glossary of Common Computer Terms

ACCESS--The ability to use computer resources such as machines, modems, printers, or software. In university environments, access to resources is a major issue, for there are never enough computing resources for all those wanting access.

ACCESSORIES--Add-on hardware for microcomputers that provides useful or interesting features. Some microcomputers come without disk drives, printers, or screens. These devices can be added onto the basic computer as accessories. Some computers can accept many accessories: extra drives, fancy printers, plotters, game devices, and other attachments. Others have only a limited selection.

ACOLYTES--The guardians of computer mysteries, often found in computer centers and in the back rooms of computer stores. They speak computerese, and although well intentioned, find it difficult to communicate their wisdom and understanding.

ADDRESS--The location of a place in the computer's memory where information is stored. By knowing the appropriate address, the microprocessor can fetch data by going directly to the addressed location in RAM.

ADEQUATE--A highly variable quantity of computing power and equipment sufficient to accomplish a range of necessary tasks. Adequate is usually less than the computer store recommends and more than you can afford.

AMUSEMENT--One of the major reasons for owning a microcomputer. Not only are the games available on some machines such as the Atari, Apple, and IBM spectacular, but programming and other computer activities provide their owners with great amusement. However, adults should never admit to purchasing a microcomputer for amusement; it will lead your colleagues to doubt your seriousness and emotional maturity.

APPLE II AND IIe--The Apple II is the technological and marketing pathbreaker of the microcomputer world. Although neither the first nor the most sophisticated machine, its exceptionally well timed introduction, its very accessible hardware, and its outstanding marketing brought microcomputing into the hands of hundreds of thousands of people who had never had close contact with computing before. The Apple II has been upgraded to something called a IIe which solves most of the technical failings of the II. Apples have a great following, especially among educators and game players, but they are also quite suitable for some serious business and research applications. The machine is characterized by its infinite adaptability and large software and hardware base.

APPLICATION--Also called application program, this is a collection of instructions for the computer that make the machine do useful work. A word processing program or a Calc is an application program. These are distinguished from operating systems or utilities that are designed to handle housekeeping chores or facilitate data manipulation but do not do real work themselves.

ARCHITECTURE--The organization, logic, and construction both of a microprocessor chip and the entire computer of which that chip forms the heart.

ASSEMBLY LANGUAGE--The instruction codes that tell the microprocessor what to do are often written in assembly language. These codes are then translated into machine language, the actual ones and zeros of computer talk. Programs prepared in assembly language have as close control over hard-

87

ware resources as is possible in most micro-computers. Assembly language programming, however, requires much knowledge about the specific hardware involved and considerable skill and patience.

BACKSPACE--For those who type, a backspace is the simple process of moving the carriage back one space so that you can type over the previous letter. This, however, is not always a trivial operation in a word processing program, and some printers are not capable of producing a true back-space. Backspacing is useful for creating strike-overs, diacriticals, boldface effects, and under-lining, although these can be created in other ways such as printing the same line twice, once with the words, the second time with the underline.

BASIC--Basic All-purpose Symbolic Instruction Code, the most widely available computer language for microcomputers, is easy to learn and use, and reasonably similar across different machines. While less well suited for applications that re-quire very complex programs or great speed, Basic is everywhere, and most computer literates try to learn a little.

BATCH--In prehistoric times, about ten years ago, most computing was done in batch mode. Instruc-tions were prepared on cards, and this batch of cards were put into a big computer that processed them and printed the results or error messages. All in its own good time. Today, batch mode is used primarily for specialized, high volume jobs. Most computing is now done interactively, with each instruction processed by the computer as it is entered. The interactive mode is much easier to use because results are very fast, learning proceeds quickly, errors are corrected immediate-ly, and the work proceeds expeditiously.

BAUD--For a variety of technical reasons, baud is not exactly equivalent to bits per second. However, advertising and amateurs have agreed that they will use baud and bits per second interchangeably, even if technically there is a difference. Baud measures the speed bits of data move along a wire or telephone line. The rates possible on microcomputers are many, but for communications over telephone lines, most microcomputers move data at either 300 or 1200 baud. Faster transmission requires better lines than normal voice telephone lines.

BIBLIOGRAPHY--Word processing programs usually have companion programs that will help prepare bibliographies from specially prepared data files to match the citations in footnotes.

BIG--A precise quantitative measure of computer memory and disk size. It refers to the memory size at least 64K units bigger than what is in your computer. It also refers to the memory of your colleague's computer if it is bigger than yours. If it is smaller, yours gets the precise qualifier of TOO BIG. Big also is used to categorize disk storage capacity. Big disks are those that hold more information than what you now have. What are big disk capacities today, by virtue of natural law, will be barely adequate tomorrow, and insufficient next week. This rule holds even if the work you need to do with those disks does not change between today and next week.

BIT--The basic unit of computer information: a one-digit value that can vary between one and zero. It is detected by the presence or absence of electrical voltage. If the voltage is there, the bit has the value of one; if not, the bit is zero. All computer operations work by manipulating many thousands of these bits.

BLOCK--Word processing programs must be capable of moving blocks of text from one place to another within a text. They also need to be able to extract a block from the text and save it to the disk in a separate file or get a block from the disk and insert it into the text. The ease with which this is accomplished varies among programs.

BOARD, ACCESSORY BOARD--Microcomputers with open buses can accept accessory boards that connect directly to the bus. These boards add a wide range of features to the microcomputer, including clocks, extra memory, RS-232-C ports, modems, and data acquisition devices. Some boards contain an additional microprocessor, and these can make an Apple, for example, behave like an IBM or an IBM behave like an Apple. Boards of this kind are called co-processor or dual-processor boards.

BOLDFACE--A special printing effect, achieved on letter-quality printers by typing a letter, spacing a fraction of a character, and restriking the same character, then moving to the next letter to repeat the process. The result is a line of words whose letters are thicker and blacker than the rest of the printed text. This feature requires a microspacing printer.

BPS--The abbreviation for bits per second as defined under Baud above.

BUG--A defect in a computer program. Bugs are very difficult to eliminate in complex programs because it is impossible to test all the conditions under which the program will be used. In the competitive market for major programs, some companies rely on users to do most of the testing. These hardy pioneers pay their own money to test a new program, find the bugs, report peculiar program behavior to the manufacturer, and sometimes receive updated and corrected versions for their trouble. The universal presence of bugs in computer programs is what prompts the advice never to buy a new program until it has been on the market six months and been through at least one major revision.

BUNDLED--In computerese, a bundled system is one that has all the parts included in the price of the equipment. If the computer is advertised as

having disks, screen, printer, and other accessories bundled into the package, that means you
get everything with the computer. Some systems
also bundle in the software. The Osborne I is a
classic case of this marketing strategy. Most
microcomputers bundle in at least the operating
system software.

BUS--The data and instruction path used to connect
the microprocessor to memory and other hardware
devices. If the bus is an open bus, the signals
are accessible through plug-in connectors, and
extra hardware can be added to the system without
rewiring or other major modifications. If the bus
is closed, then the machine is fixed pretty much
as it is delivered and expansion or modification
will require major surgery if it can be done at
all. Much of the success of the Apple II can be
traced to its open bus. The IBM PC also has an
open bus.

BYTE--A collection of eight bits. Because the
microcomputer explosion took place on machines
using 8-bit microprocessors, the byte has been
consecrated as the fundamental unit of microcomputer information. A 16-bit microprocessor
works with two bytes at a time. For those interested in jargon, half a byte, that is, four bits,
is called a nibble. BYTE is also the name of the
major monthly microcomputer magazine, known for
its technical construction articles, enthusiastic
support of new technology, and massive amounts of
advertising.

CALC--A shorthand term for the electronic spreadsheet program. This name comes from the trade-
marks of some of the most popular examples of
these programs such as VisiCalc or SuperCalc.

CHARACTER--A number, letter, or code that the computer can recognize. Most microcomputers recognize
at least the 128 characters that are called the
ASCII (American Standard Code for Information
Interchange) character code. These codes or char-

91

acters can each be made up out of seven bits and
therefore work well for microcomputers. Most
microcomputers interpret these 128 characters in
exactly the same way, but they do different things
with a second set of 128 characters that can be
created by using the eighth bit in the microcomputer byte. The difference is not very important
for most users except for communications and word
processing. Some communications devices will only
accept the first 128 characters and if you send
something from the second 128, the computer will
convert them automatically to their counterpart in
the first 128. Because word processing programs
frequently use all 256 codes, you may need to be
sure you are going to have 8-bit ASCII file transfers if you expect to move word processing files.
A 7-bit transfer won't do because it will only
give you 128 characters.

CHIP--The generic name for all the integrated circuits in your microcomputer. The main chip, of
course, is the microprocessor. It has a bunch of
support chips that help manage memory and external
devices such as keyboards and screens. Memory,
too, is composed of memory chips. Some chips are
quite susceptible to static electricity damage, so
if you feel like changing or replacing chips, be
sure you touch an electrical ground before
handling any computer chips.

CLONE--Another name for a look-alike computer. A
clone is supposed to imply even closer compatibility between the original and the copy, but the
two terms are used interchangeably.

CLUBS--Special interest computer clubs are useful
places for information. Most are organized around
specific machines or families of machines. Direc-
tories of clubs are available from retailers,
universities, computer magazines, and computer
manufacturers.

CODE--In addition to its normal meaning, code is
often used to refer to the symbolic instructions

in a computer program. To write code means to prepare a computer program using the symbolic instructions appropriate to that programming language.

COMMANDS--The instructions that a program or application requires to start, finish, or continue a process. For example, to discover what is on the disk drive, you must issue the command that asks the operating system to list the disk directory to the screen. Computer commands usually have to be typed exactly as specified in the manuals, or the machine will not understand them.

COMMUNICATION--All the many activities involved in exchanging information between computers and associated devices. The microcomputer can communicate with a printer, a modem, or another computer. Communications can take place between two machines or through a network among many machines. Communications, while simple in theory, requires a careful match between hardware and software if it is to work easily.

COMPATIBILITY--The bane of microcomputer technology. Very few things in the microcomputer world are totally compatible. Always assume incompatibility between machines, software, disks, and communications equipment until proven otherwise. Technological innovation and marketing strategies appear to be increasing incompatibilities in this industry.

COMPILER--The program that takes high-level programming code and translates it into the ones and zeros the computer understands. The compiled program is saved as a file, and when the program is run, the machine reads the ones and zeros. If there is an error, the original program must be fixed and then recompiled into the corrected ones and zeros.

CP/M--The most important operating system for 8-bit microcomputers, CP/M stands for Control Program Microprocessor and is the work of a company called

Digital Research.

CPU—Central Processing Unit. In large computers, the CPU often exists as a separate entity within the computer, supported by other devices. In a microcomputer the CPU is part of the microprocessor which also performs a variety of other functions. Some writers use CPU as a synonym for microprocessor when speaking of microcomputers.

CRASH—When a computer system fails in the midst of a task, it is said to have crashed. A crash is frequently accompanied by a total loss of whatever information was in the computer at the time of the crash.

CURSOR—The box or underline that blinks at you from the screen and tells you where the next character you type will appear. Some systems use the shape of the cursor to tell you what activity is in process.

DAISY WHEEL—A type element for letter-quality printers consisting of a rimless wheel composed of 90 to 100 spokes. Each spoke, like the petal of a daisy, is flexible. At the end of each spoke is a letter or symbol that when hit by the printer's hammer transfers the character impression through the ribbon onto the paper. Daisy wheels come in many type styles and with a wide variety of character sets.

DATA FILE—A collection of information stored on a disk. These files are distinguished in most systems from program files which are sequences of instructions. The maximum size of a data file permitted on a disk is an important indication of data processing capacity. Data files are usually organized into subgroups of information called records, which can be further subdivided into fields. Applications programs that use data files usually provide special instructions about how these files are to be organized and kept.

DEDICATED—A special purpose device is called a dedicated device. For example, a microcomputer

94

built to do nothing but process words is called a
dedicated word processor. Most microcomputers are
general purpose devices, but in industry there is
still a considerable market for dedicated devices.

DEVICE--Computerese for any gadget that can be
attached to a computer.

DIAL-UP--The description of a computer that can be
accessed by dialing the telephone. A dial-up
system is a computer setup that has a special
modem that will answer the phone and connect itself to the calling computer so an exchange of
information can take place. A dial-up system is
accessible to anyone with the proper phone number,
a compatible computer, and the required passwords.

DIRECT CONNECT--A modem that plugs directly into the
telephone network with a wire instead of through
an acoustic coupler that uses the earphone and
mouthpiece of the telephone is called a direct
connect modem.

DIALECTS--The various versions of a computer language. Basic, Pascal, and every other standard
computer language come in dialects that reflect
the sophistication and power of the microcomputer
on which they are installed. While Basic on the
Apple and Basic on the IBM PC are very similar in
structure and vocabulary, there are significant
differences in syntax and special instructions
that make it impossible to run an Apple Basic
program directly on an IBM or vice versa. These,
then, are two dialects of Basic.

DICTIONARY--The word list used by a spelling program. The size of this dictionary is usually
limited by the capacity of the disks used by the
system. Most microcomputer dictionaries are in
the 20,000 to 80,000 word range. Most spellers
will permit multiple dictionaries to be used, thus
permitting the creation of special technical dictionaries for specialized documents.

DIRECTORY--The file on a microcomputer disk that
contains information about all the other files on

95

the disk. The directory tells the computer where
each file resides, how much information is there,
and how much room is left on the disk. It also
keeps track of the names used to identify each of
the files and some other housekeeping information.
If the directory is damaged or scrambled, the disk
is unreadable by normal means.

DISCOUNT--What everyone gets when they buy a microcomputer. The size of the discount depends on
whether you purchase in bulk or individually.
Institutional discounts can be substantial.
Reported discounts from friends and relatives tend
to be larger than what real people can get at
actual stores. What people tell you they got in
the way of a discount is roughly proportional to
the size of the fish that got away.

DISK AND DISK DRIVE--The principal components of the
microcomputer's external storage system. Disks
and disk drives are of two major types: floppy
disks and drives and hard disks and drives. A
floppy disk is flexible, removable, and susceptible to dirt, dust, and environmental hazards.
It is, however, cheap and reasonably reliable.
Hard disks are rigid, operate in sealed environments away from environmental contamination, store
great amounts of information, and are quite expensive. Hard disks usually can transfer data much
faster from the disk to the computer's memory and
back than the floppy disks.

DISPLAY SCREEN--This is the principal way most users
interact with their computers. What you type in
and the computer's responses appear on this
screen. Screens come attached, separate, large,
small, and various colors. Quality is often more
a subjective judgment than a technical judgment.
European designers think amber is the color of
choice for monochrome video display screens used
with computers. Many in the United States and
elsewhere like green screens. Traditionalists
like black and white screens. There is a large

and growing literature designed to tell you which is best for your eyes and general mental and visual health. Unfortunately, this literature is inconclusive and contradictory. An amateur will tell you to get the screen you think looks pretty and doesn't give you a headache. Color monitors or screens take a signal from the computer and translate it into color images on the screen. Color monitors come in many sizes and prices. The higher the price, the higher the resolution. Resolution refers to the sharpness of the image that can be shown and is usually quoted in terms of number of points that can be put on the screen horizontally or vertically. Color monitors also come in two major varieties in the US. Composite monitors use one signal from the computer that has all the color information combined. These monitors are cheaper, as a rule, and have lower quality resolution and color. RGB (Red Green Blue) monitors receive a separate signal for each of these primary colors, and as a result have clearer and sharper color images. They are correspondingly more expensive.

DOCUMENT--The text you expect to edit and print. Some word processors reserve the word document to refer to text that will be formatted especially and use text to refer to lists and other material that will be printed exactly as it is entered with no rearranging done by the computer.

DOS--Disk Operating System. The general supervisory program for operating a microcomputer with all of its hardware attachments and software programs. The most popular DOS for microcomputers is CP/M, but there are many other good operating systems.

DOT MATRIX PRINTERS--Versatile, fast, and often inexpensive printers that form characters and symbols out of a matrix of dots, commonly 7 dots across and 9 dots high. These printers can be programmed to produce any characters or symbols or draw graphics images. While the quality of letters produced by these printers is not quite as good as those from a letter-quality printer, they are much more versatile.

DOWNLOAD--The process of moving a file of information or a program from a main frame computer to a microcomputer. This can be done over telephone lines or hard wired lines.

DUMB TERMINAL--A keyboard and screen combination whose only purpose is to communicate with a computer. It is usually not a computer and has none of the computing power. However, a microcomputer can be programmed to behave like a dumb terminal and operate in conjunction with a main frame computer. This facilitates work with the main frame that may expect special characters generated by a particular brand of dumb terminal.

EDITOR--The part of a word processing program that accepts text, modifies text, and saves text.

ELECTRONIC MAIL--A message service maintained on a computer that permits sending and receiving private messages between computers or computer terminals. The electronic mail system can be used with a direct or hard wired network or with a dial-up network.

ENHANCEMENT--Something special added onto an existing program or hardware device. Frequently a marketing gimmick designed to convince you that the old stuff is new. Also used by software suppliers to explain some peculiarity in their program that was missed in testing but is too expensive to fix. This peculiarity, if it doesn't actually destroy the program, is called an enhancement.

ERROR--What the software people say is caused by the hardware and what the hardware people say is caused by the software. If pressed, both groups usually can agree that error is caused by the user.

EXPANDABLE--A computer that has an open bus and can accept a variety of expansion cards or accessory boards is said to be expandable. Some computers that can accept extra printers or disk drives but don't have open buses also advertise themselves as expandable.

EXPERT--Someone who has had a computer two months longer than you have.

FIELD--A subset of information within a record.

FILE--See Data File.

FLOPPY--Shorthand for floppy disk.

FONTS--In typesetting, the different styles and sizes of typefaces available to the printer. Many microcomputer printers have the capability of generating or using a number of different fonts to produce widely varied printed effects.

FORMATTER--A program that takes text prepared on an editor and rearranges it to fit nicely on the page. The formatter handles paragraphs, under-lines, justification, pagination, headers and footers, and all other characteristics of the document's final appearance.

FORTH--A powerful special purpose computer language that is fast, efficient, hard to read, and rela-tively difficult to learn.

GENERATION--The time between the introduction of one kind of microcomputer and the introduction of a significantly improved machine. If the Apple II was one generation and the IBM PC is the next generation, then a generation is about three or four years. However, the life span of equipment is much longer than a generation, perhaps three times as long.

GRAPHICS--Computerese for all shapes and pictures that are not letters and numbers. Graphics normally refers to the microcomputer's ability to draw pictures, graphs, pie charts, diagrams, and other arbitrary shapes. Microcomputer capabili-ties in this area vary widely, with business graphics and game graphics the most prevalent and well developed applications.

HANDSHAKE--The protocol or pattern of signals exchanged between computers or computer and attached device to indicate when each is ready to send and receive information.

HARD DISK--See Disk.

HARDWARE--The machinery, the tangible goods of the computer business. Hardware, although it is the easiest to appreciate because it is there, is useless without the software or programs, which are less easy to appreciate because they exist only in electronic form.

HARD WIRED--A hard wired network or system connects the machines in the network through wires that run between the various machines. Frequently universities will permit access to their equipment both through hard wired connections and dial-up connections. Hard wired also refers to changes and modifications that are made to computer equipment that actually permanently change the machine as opposed to plug in changes with accessory boards.

HOST COMPUTER--When you use a terminal with a main frame computer, the main frame is called the host. Also used to refer to the main frame when communicating with a microcomputer.

HOUSEKEEPING--All the activities related to managing hardware resources, keeping track of files, handling screen displays, and the other little chores required to keep the system in order. Most housekeeping is done by the operating system.

IBM PC--One of the most interesting microcomputers on the market today, in part because of the muscle of its parent company, and second only to the Apple II in terms of the impact it has had and will have on the industry. The machine itself is an open bus, versatile, and adaptable machine. It uses a 16-bit microprocessor, and can directly address a megabyte of memory, but it uses an 8-bit bus so that it fetches information in smaller chunks. The result is a compromise machine that because it is well positioned in the market has generated tremendous support.

100

IMPLEMENTATION--This, in computerese, means to make an idea or a program work in a specific situation or with a particular machine. If I have a word processor that works on my Apple and I buy an IBM, I write the company that makes the word processor and ask if they have an implementation of the program for the IBM.

INCOMPATIBILITY--The natural state of microcomputer hardware and software.

INPUT--Information that goes to the microprocessor.

INTELLIGENT TERMINAL--Unlike a dumb terminal, an intelligent terminal can do a number of functions without asking the host computer for help. It can frequently manage a whole screen or several screens of information without calling the host computer. If a host expects an intelligent terminal, it will not work well or sometimes at all with a dumb one. Many communications programs for microcomputers will make the micro operate like any one of a number of popular intelligent terminals.

INTERACTIVE COMPUTING--The opposite of batch computing. Interactive means that each instruction or action at the keyboard is immediately processed by the computer so that you can interact with the machine.

INTERNAL MEMORY--Refers to the RAM and ROM directly accessed by the computer. Usually used to distinguish disk drives, cassette tapes, or other external storage devices from RAM and ROM.

INTERPRETED LANGUAGES--High level languages are interpreted when each instruction is converted to ones and zeros every time it is encountered. The computer operates directly on the instructions in sequence, and each time the program is run, the conversion from instruction to ones and zeros takes place. Thus interpreted languages tend to run more slowly but are easier to work with, especially for short programs. Basic is usually available on microcomputers as an interpreted

language.

JUSTIFIED--Text that has an even right margin. Justification can be done by adding whole spaces between words or by adding microspaces. Microspaced justification has a much better appearance but requires a more expensive printer.

K--An abbreviation for 1,024 in computer talk. Used as if it referred to 1,000. Thus a kilobyte is equal to 1,024 bytes.

LETTER QUALITY--Printers that print with formed characters similar to regular typewriters.

LITERACY--The ability to read computer manuals, understand computer operations, and make computers work for you.

LOCAL NETWORK--A collection of computers connected together directly by wires. Local networks are usually restricted to relatively limited geographic areas such as a single office building. The technology for connecting local networks is different from what is required for a large, telephone based network.

LOOK-ALIKE--A jargon name for computers of one manufacturer that are designed to work just like the computers of another manufacturer. Most look-alikes are designed to copy the functions of either Apples, IBMs, or Radio Shack computers. Truly compatible look-alikes will accept all software and all hardware designed to operate with the original. Most, but not all, look-alikes fail this test.

MAGNETIC COATING--The thin film of material on a disk's surface that preserves the information transmitted by the computer to the disk drive. The quality of the magnetic coating has a great deal to do with the amount of information that can be kept on a disk.

MAIN FRAME--A large computer. The distinction between microcomputers, minicomputers, and main frames has become blurred at the boundaries between the categories. Computer scientists

classify these machines according to memory size, processing speed, and internal architecture, among other criteria. A main frame computer will be many orders of magnitude bigger and more powerful than a micro.

MAINTENANCE--The aspect of microcomputing most often neglected. There is very little sex-appeal to maintenance, and because most of the microcomputers in service now are only a few years old, the true dimensions of the maintenance problem have yet to be discovered. One consequence of low unit prices for machines and the high cost of maintenance will be throwaway computers, machines with a predicted life span of three years that are designed to be discarded at the end of that time and replaced with a new and better model.

MEDIUM--In computer talk this usually refers to the kind of storage involved. Thus most microcomputers receive their software through the medium of 5-1/4" floppy disks. But software is also provided through the medium of ROM, read only memory, or larger disks such as 8". Medium also refers to the way the disks are recorded. An advertisement for software may claim that programs come on media compatible with IBM, Apple, and CP/M. Although all three may use 5-1/4" disks, they do not record the information in exactly the same way.

MEGABYTES--One thousand kilobytes, or something over a million bytes.

MICRO--Short for microcomputer.

MICROCOMPUTER--A computer built around a microprocessor.

MICROPROCESSOR--The complex integrated circuit that serves as the central processing unit of a microcomputer. Main frame acolytes call these, with great disdain, plastic processors because they come embedded in a plastic case. Microprocessors are classified by the number of bits they can handle at one time. An 8-bit machine works with a maximum of 8 bits at once, and by virtue of its

design can directly address only about 64,000
memory locations. A 16-bit machine has a much
greater capacity and can directly address about 1
million memory locations. When an additional
microprocessor is installed in the computer it can
operate as a co-processor or a dual-processor.
Generally a co-processor works with the main processor and a dual-processor replaces the main
processor.

MICROSOFT--The producer of the most prevalent Basic
dialects used in microcomputers. Also the producer of the operating system used in the IBM PC,
known as MS-DOS.

MICROSPACES--Letter quality printers can microspace
if they can move the carriage in fractions of an
inch, usually about 1/120 of an inch. If your
printer can micospace you will get good boldfaced
print and better looking justified margins. You
can also, with the appropriate software, get proportional spacing.

MODEM--A modulator-demodulator which modulates a
computer signal so it can pass through the telephone system and then demodulates it at the other
end so the receiving computer can understand the
information. This device is necessary to access
the many computer networks that operate via dial-
up systems.

MONITOR--The display screen connected to the computer. Monitor is also used to refer to the small
computer program inside the machine stored in ROM
that the microprocessor runs whenever it is turned
on. Some microcomputers have monitors with useful
routines included, but others only use the monitor
to get the machine ready to load in programs
stored externally on disk.

MYLAR--The plastic used in manufacturing floppy
disks as the base material for the magnetic
coating.

NET--Shorthand for network.

NETWORK--Any connected group of computers, whether

linked by telephone or directly wired one to the other.

NONREMOVABLE--This refers to the disk inside a hard disk drive. Most hard disks are nonremovable, but there are rigid disk drives that use special cartridges that hold the hard disk which can be removed. Main frame hard disk drives are frequently removable, but also very expensive.

NONSTANDARD--Almost everything in the microcomputer business.

OBSOLESCENT--The normal condition of computer hardware and especially of microcomputer hardware.

OPERATING SYSTEM--The collection of programs and routines that manage the microcomputer's hardware resources: disk drives, screen, keyboard, memory, and accessories. Most programs gain access to hardware resources through the operating system.

OUTPUT--Whatever the microprocessor sends to the outside world. Output can be printed, displayed on a screen, sent to a plotting device, or appear as musical tones.

PACKAGE--An integrated collection of programs or routines that serve a particular need or application. Statistical packages, for example, have many statistical formulas built in, all of which use data that is entered and prepared in a standard format.

PARALLEL PORT--A connection between computer and external device that transfers data 8 bits at a time using a cable with more than 8 wires. Frequently used to connect dot matrix printers and microcomputers.

PASCAL--A very elegant and useful computer language that is believed to teach good programming habits. The implementation called UCSD Pascal is very popular in the microcomputing world. However, there are a number of other important dialects of Pascal for microcomputers.

PLOTTER--A device for drawing lines, graphs, and figures of all kinds. Plotters usually work with one or more pens that can be moved over the paper in any direction under computer control, and can produce very elaborate designs. Some smaller plotters are within the reach of microcomputer enthusiasts and sell for about the price of a medium quality dot matrix printer.

PORT--A computer port is a connection into the internal hardware of the machine. The most common port on a microcomputer is a communications port, usually set up to conform to the RS-232-C standard for serial communications. However, other ports to connect special devices are also available. Computers without open buses must attach all external devices through these ports. Ports usually do not provide direct access to the microcomputer bus.

PRINTER--Although it is possible to operate a microcomputer without a printer, it really makes little sense except for very special purposes.

PRINTOUT--What the computer sends out to the printer and the printer prints.

PROGRAM--The sequence of instructions that make the computer do useful work.

PROGRAMMING LANGUAGE--The symbolic instruction codes prepared by a programmer that tell the computer what to do. High level programming languages such as Basic or Pascal have codes and procedures that are relatively easy to read and understand. They require translation either by an interpreter or a compiler so the machine can read them in the appropriate ones and zeros. Low level programming languages such as Assembler use codes that are much closer to the machine's ones and zeros but are harder to use and read.

PROMPTS--Lines, symbols, or letters that indicate what type of information the program requires from the operator or that tells what activity is currently in process. Computers with informative prompts are often called user-friendly.

PROPORTIONAL SPACING--The ability to give each

printed character the amount of space it needs but no more. Thus the l and the i would get less space on the line than an m or a w. Proportional spacing requires special software and a micro-spacing printer to be successful.

P-SYSTEM--A type of generic operating system that is especially useful for Pascal programming environments, although it will support other programming languages as well.

RADIO SHACK--Manufacturer of the very popular TRS-80 line of microcomputers. With Apple, one of the pioneers in the microcomputer revolution. Known for its closed approach to hardware and its ubiquitous stores throughout the United States. Radio Shack has always used closed bus computer designs and discouraged the development of attachments to its machines by outside companies.

RAM--Random Access Memory. This is the memory that can be used to store and retrieve, write and read, data or instructions. Most microcomputers should have 64K of this RAM as a minimum. Many will easily take 128K to 256K.

READ--Refers to the process of copying data from storage, either in memory or on a disk, and bringing it to where the program can use it. Reading data is usually not a destructive process and most often really means copying the data from where it is stored to where it will be used.

RECORD--A record is a subdivision of a computer file. A file can have one record or many records, but each operating system has a set of rules about how it tells where a file starts and stops and what separates the records within each file.

RESOURCE--Computerese for a computer hardware device. Disks, screens, memory, and printers are all resources. A shared resource is one that several computers can use, such as a large hard disk.

ROM--Read Only Memory. This is memory that has prewritten instructions or data. This memory can only be read or copied; it cannot be written.

ROUTINES--These are usually program fragments or
short programs that accomplish useful things. A
sorting routine, for example, sorts data into
alphabetical order.

RS-232-C--The name of a set of specifications that
serves as a standard for communications between
two computer devices. RS-232-C is used to connect
serial devices, such as printers and modems and
plotters. It is capable of sending and receiving
data at a variety of speeds, but it cannot work
over long distances. An RS-232-C interface is
often called a Standard Serial Interface.

RUN--Programs are run when they are put into operation. They run, or operate, until they finish or
encounter a bug. If they encounter a bug, they
may crash. Then they must be fixed and run again.

SCREEN--See Display Screen.

SEARCH--The function in a word processing program
that will seek out a particular word, phrase, or
combination of characters. Sometimes called
Find. Often combined with a Replace function that
will find the characters and replace them with
some other characters. Every word processor
should have these features.

SERIAL--A method of sending data in which the bits
are shipped down the wire one at a time in a
series. The rules for this form of transmission
vary, but the most prevalent standard for serial
communication is RS-232-C.

SOFTWARE--The programs that make the microcomputer
useful.

SOURCE CODE--The instructions of a computer program
before they are interpreted or compiled into ones
and zeros. While it is relatively easy to modify
a program if you have the source code, if all you
have are the ones and zeros (known as the object
code) it is almost impossible to modify the program. Software companies often refuse to release
the source code to prevent others from stealing

the programming tricks used in their software.

SPEED--Every computer can be classified by the speed with which it carries out certain kinds of instructions. However, for microcomputers, speed tests are not always very good indicators of the amount of time it will take to complete a task. Speed tests are mostly useful if your application involves many repetitive operations using standard procedures, for example, processing large pay-rolls. For general purpose computing, speed is a relatively minor consideration. However, for certain scientific applications where the computer is supposed to collect information from experi-ments, the machine must be fast enough to collect the data as it comes in.

SPELLER--A companion program to word processors. Spellers do much more than catch spelling errors, and some will analyze text and correct punctua-tion. See Dictionary.

SPREADSHEET--What is called a Calc program in this book. Spreadsheet programs offer an electronic spreadsheet of many columns and rows capable of handling complex relationships between the rows and columns.

SPSS--Statistical Package for the Social Sciences. One of the most popular statistical packages available on main frame computers.

STRIKEOVER--Good printers need to be capable of striking one character on top of another in order to get underlining, diacritical markings, and similar effects. Some strikeovers are done by backspacing, and some are done by retyping the same line.

TERMINALS--See Dumb Terminal, Intelligent Terminal.

TEXT--The material entered into a word processing system and manipulated by the editor and format-ter. It can be documents or program source code, or anything that will not be handled mathemati-cally. If you expect to add things up, then you are not dealing with text. If you are listing

numbers in a report then those numbers become
text.

TRACK--Disk information resides on concentric
tracks. Different disk drives use different numbers of tracks per disk. One or more of these
tracks is reserved for the disk directory.

TRANSFER--Usually, the movement of data from the
computer to some external device. You can read
about the transfer speed of information from disk
drive to computer memory or you can hear about a
communications program's ability to transfer files
from a microcomputer to a main frame.

TRANSPORTABILITY--A program written on one machine
is transportable if it will run on another machine
made by a different manufacturer. Very few programs are entirely transportable, and much effort
is directed toward changing programs written on
one computer so that they can be transported to
another.

TRS-80--The name for the line of microcomputers
manufactured by Radio Shack.

TYPESETTING--One of the growing uses for microcompu-
ter-based word processors is the preparation of
text for input into a typesetter which can then
prepare printed copy that looks as if it had been
set by hand. As the costs of typesetting rise,
more and more publishers want to receive manuscripts in a computer readable form that permits
the addition of special typesetting codes.

UCSD--University of California San Diego, the owners
of the computer operating system known as the UCSD
P-system and the version of Pascal that runs under
this operating system.

UPDATES--The corrections, improvements, and addi-
tions to software programs that a good software
company will send to all the purchasers of the
original package. The availability of updates is
an important consideration in choosing software
packages.

UPLOAD--Refers to the process of transferring data

110

or files from a microcomputer to a main frame computer.

USER--Anyone who has and uses a computer.

UTILITY--A program whose function is to help with the housekeeping chores. Frequently includes programs to repair disks, to rearrange files, to handle special hardware configurations, to convert data from one format to another, and in general do preparation and clean-up work.

VERSION--Software and hardware are continually being revised. You need to be aware of the version number of your major equipment and programs so you can tell whether your version is the latest and whether other programs and devices will work with your versions of equipment and programs.

VOLATILE--Refers to memory whose content disappears when the computer power is turned off. Most RAM is volatile.

WORD PROCESSING--The combination of editing and formatting that facilitates the preparation of text and documents. The universal use for micro-computers.

WRITE--The process of putting information into memory or onto a disk. This is a destructive process because it erases whatever was located at the place where the new information is put. RAM memory can be written to, but ROM cannot.

Index

This index covers the main text. Material in the Glossary is already organized alphabetically.

Adults, and Microcomputers, 1-8
Applications Languages, 60-64
Apple Computers, 12, 13, 20, 21, 67
Assembly Language, 60

Basic Computer Language, 59-60
Baud, 46
Bit, 11
Boldface, 29
Bus, 13
Byte, 11

Calc, 39-42
Camera Ready, 35-36
Children and Microcomputers, 3-4, 5
Communications, 43-53; Diagram of, 47;
  Programs, 46, 48; Protocols, 48-49
Compiled Languages, 58-59
Computer Literacy, defined, 1-8; How to
  Acquire, 72-85
CP/M, 19-20, 67

Data Base Packages, 61
Data Files, 22
Dictionaries, 31

Educational Discount Available

Computer Literacy may be used as an introductory textbook to the concepts and language of computer technology. Bulk purchases of 5 or more paperback copies will qualify for a special 25% educational discount.

To order, or for more information

Call collect:
(812) 335-6657

or write to:

Indiana University Press
Dept. CL
10th & Morton Streets
Bloomington, IN 47405

<u>Institutions</u>:
Include purchase order number, name, institution, address, city, state, and zip code. Institutional orders will be invoiced when accompanied by a purchase order number.

<u>Individuals</u>:
Include name, address, city, state, and zip code. Prepayment is required. Send check payable to Indiana University Press or use MasterCard or VISA. To determine amount due, multiply quantity (5 or more copies) by $4.46 ($5.95 less 25%) and add $0.25 per copy for postage and handling. Indiana residents add 5% sales tax.